W9-AAV-682

Ernest L. Norman
Author, philosopher, poet, scientist, director,
moderator of Unarius Science of Life.

UNARIUS
UNiversal ARticulate Interdimensional

Understanding of Science

THE PULSE OF CREATION SERIES

Volume II

THE VOICE OF EROS

THE

VOICE OF EROS

Clairvoyantly received

by

ERNEST L. NORMAN

The Second *Volume of*

THE PULSE OF CREATION

Second Edition

Published By
UNARIUS, SCIENCE OF LIFE
P.O. Box 1042
El Cajon, CA 92020

Copyright © 1958 by Ernest L. and Ruth E. Norman

ISBN 0-932642-01-2

Printed and published in the United States of America

By

Ruth E. Norman

(Listed in the order in which they have given transmissions throughout the "Pulse of Creation" Series:)

Nikola Tesla
Leonardo da Vinci
Eliason
Faraday
Kung Fu
Shakespeare
Krishna
Elizabeth & Robt. Browning
Robert Louis Stevenson
Gamaliel
Fred Nietzsche
Helena P. Blavatsky
Lao-tze
Copernicus
Leeuwenhoek
Galileo
William James
Charles Pearce
Darwin
Isaac Newton
Luther Burbank
Plutarch (of Chaeronea)
Christian Huygens
Buddha
Maitreya
Athena
Kuthumi
William Crookes
Volta

Hippocrates
Pythagoras
Meng-tse
Swedenborg
Louis Pasteur
Washington Irving
Plato
Hermes
Moira (Blavatsky's teacher)
Asoka
St. Theresa
Benjamin Franklin
Abe Lincoln
Mozart
Omar Khayyam
Dwal Khul
Zoroaster
Rene' Descartes
Dratzel
Lord Calvin
Carrie Jacobs Bond
St. Patrick
Mahatma Gandhi
Moses
Mohammed
St. Francis of Assisi
Archangel Uriel
Sha-tok (Jesus of Nazareth)

CHAPTER 31

Greetings from Eros! First, let me introduce myself. For convenience sake, I can be called Nikola, as I once lived on your earth planet some years ago and was known as Nikolas Tesla. I might say that many of your inventions in electricity and of other things came to you earth people through the channel of my mind; and while this is of small importance inasmuch as all of the modern conveniences and the wonders of your present-day world have come to you from this planet, I would like to say that we here do not assume any burdens of responsibility for the misuse and misunderstanding in applying the knowledge and wisdom which has been given you.

As you were told, from the previous book of Venus, there are actually seven portions called Shamballa, and that they relate in their particular aspect to seven different dimensions of expression. On the planet Venus, they express their relationship to you in the field of spiritual therapy and with the adjustments and various other factors which enter into man's spiritual evolution. As we continue in the explanation in the various other books, it will become apparent to you that the evolution or reincarnation of mankind, individually and collectively, assumes vast and staggering proportions. It was previously pointed out to you that such evolution was something of a spiraling staircase. I might say too, that you might liken it to a great wheel with many spokes, that you appeared and reappeared countless numbers of times around the outer periphery of this wheel; and that the hub was actually the God-Force or Fountainhead, as it was called, wherein stemmed all of the Radiant Energies from and to the many dimensions and planes of expressions. It was in your traveling around this giant circumference that you would be able to view and gain wisdom and knowledge in your relationship with the God-Force that would ultimately expand your consciousness into abstract proportions whereby you could gain a complete and introspective view of all things.

As in the case, however, of all people who are reactionary in nature such as your earth plane people, it is often customary to go off balance; by so lacking the proper proportion of introspection, they may manifest an off balance or an overbalance of certain values. Your pages of history will relate you and show you how this has been done through your many pages of time. In your present day, you are expressing a preponderance of materialism. However, this too shall pass and you will pass into another age where you will express a preponderance of your spiritual nature. These, in themselves, are factors which will, as I have said, relate you eventually to a true introspective place in your evolution.

As on Venus, we are expressing ourselves in a particular dimension wherein there are various and multiple factors whereby you can distinguish such things in your earth life; for instance, we might say that color was also expressed here just as it was on Venus. There their particular color relationship was of the blue nature; here it is of the white. While, of course, in all of these dimensions there is a great deal of what is called color; however, the relationship of what is called color here is different than it is on your earth plane. I would like to point out that the translation of color on your particular planes means the quality of absorption or reflection from the various energy masses with which you are surrounded. Nothing in itself contains color, as you would so think but only has its own property of reflecting a particular part of your color spectrum. You have many people on your earth plane who are partially or wholly color blind; they do not have the proper value of perception which will relate them to the vibrations of energy which you call color. So color in itself merely means a preponderance of energy which has been expressed in a particular direction. Such energy, as it fills the void which you call space, is of a pulsating radiant nature and supersedes all values of your known color spectrums. I would also like to say that I am going to keep these discussions down to a level of understanding that can be accepted by the greatest number of people. However, our dimension here is purely scientific and relates man with God in the scientific nature or aspect of His being. Such a relationship as pure science is, of course, vital and essential to his spiritual evolution and introspective position.

Going directly to our planet of Eros, I would like to say that we alone, of the seven Shamballas, have an unfixed position; in other words, we travel in an elliptical orbit which comes in contact with a large number of planets which are similar to your earth. We make this orbit about once every 3800 years in your earth time. By dividing this into half, you will see that we will come into position, either exactly opposite your earth or exactly in its affinity in this proportion.

About 2000 years ago, you saw our planet over a certain portion of the earth which has been called the

Holy Land. Many people saw the planet at that time although it is not generally visible by any known astronomical or astrophysical means, as we here are in a dimension or relationship which is not reactive to your sense of sight. However, at that time, it was necessary to make a very close contact with the earth for various purposes. Great infusions of radiant energy were projected from our planet at that time which permeated and infused the minds of many earth people which made possible the many miracles of the Master Jesus.

It was He who had served his apprenticeship and mastery on this planet which enabled him to go to your earth plane and perform the many miracles in the spiritual sense in which they were performed. If you will also recall, He spoke of the many other miracles which would be worked on the earth plane at a different time. (Greater things than these shall ye do also.) In this He was, of course, referring to the many things which you have about you today.

As on Venus, we too have many levels of expression some of which are not, in a proper sense, the very highest or the purest values of science if we can use the word high or pure. Many times individuals will reincarnate or appear in these lower levels and after receiving some instruction and scholastic abilities, will reincarnate into your earth plane through their own will and dominion and thus reproduce many of the scientific inventions and knowledge which they learned here. Thus it is sometimes that knowledge is given to your earth plane which is not conducive to the best way of life, or that many of these inventions and appurtenances can sometimes be destructively or selfishly used.

There is in your present age a great number of these mechanical and electronic inventions which, in a more pure esoterical sense of relationship, should have given mankind on your earth plane a greater freedom and understanding of life. Now they have become a burden, one in which you must all struggle for the bare necessities of life. Thus it is that you shall learn through the evolutions of time that while there is a difference between knowledge and wisdom, it is one thing to know of something but it is not wisdom until such knowledge is properly applied. So it is through the age which you now call your atomic age.

Let us now go directly to our planet and obtain our first view of the fifth spiritual plane of Shamballa which is the scientific plane. Now we find ourselves sitting on what apparently looks like a mountain top; and while you are looking at the substance upon which you are sitting as something similar in shape and form to your familiar earth planet as rock, yet it possesses some peculiar transparency or brilliance to which you are unaccustomed. As in the case of Venus, all elemental substances are in a much higher state of evolution than your earth planet. This principle of evolution was somewhat explained to you and in a more proper understanding of this principle, you will begin to understand that there is nothing happenstance or by chance in God's great Celestial universe, but is all a thoroughly and completely integrated relationship. And so it is with the things around you on your earth plane; your mountains, your trees, your streams, your lakes, your cities, and so on, are all just a very small fragment of manifestation of the Infinite Mind. If you will think a moment, you can see that this same manifestation will take place on and on, up into many, many other dimensions which are completely foreign to your understanding. Thus it is with Venus, and so it is with us and numerous other great planets and solar systems throughout the universe.

The astronomer or astrophysicist looks through the telescope and sees what is apparently a vast mass of unrelated stars and star systems. While some may appear as nebulae or star clusters in such shapes as may be likened to a pinwheel, others appear as cloud masses. He may think this is rather an ordinary circumstance, whereby they seem to have been tossed by a giant hand out into the sky, but this is not so. If he were clairvoyant, he would see that around all of these star clusters and various galaxies, that there was a definitely related pattern which extended through many other dimensions. So it is with Eros; while we, in a sense, can and do sometimes direct our planet as it best suits our needs, yet as I have said, we do travel in an orbit. This we have been able to accomplish simply because of very high values in our relationship with the Infinite emanating Source of radiant energy.

Now that we are sitting here upon this mountain top, I see you are looking out upon the planes below you, that you are seeing what looks to you like a giant wheel, and that this presents a very strange appearance to you. And while the whole world about you seems to be glowing and pulsating with a white radiant energy, yet as you will become more accustomed to this, you will, as you did on Venus, see that it is a planet which is composed of many hundreds of different kinds of pulsating or radiant energies. What appears to you to be a vast wheel is a city; the center hub is, of course, like a more familiar earth plane equation of the wheel, the center or the controlling force of this whole city. Through the many spokes and out into the rim which covers the plane for many miles in all directions are, shall I say, buildings which are constructed, just as in Venus, of the radiant energies which have been somewhat crystallized or held in form and shape.

The difference here, however, is that these seemingly solid crystalline structures reside in a somewhat different dimension, and therefore possess somewhat different qualities. The buildings in themselves are very beautiful and streamlined and modernistic in appearance and in all cases as you will walk through the various corridors or spokes, and into the various other portions of this huge and vast city, you will find that there are great centers and laboratories. There you will find that they are teaching countless thousands of souls or individuals not only your earth plane experience, but of many other earth plane experiences. Many of these souls, I might say, are being taught for some future day when they will make their appearance in some other earth-like planet to teach a new science, or they may be people who are from your own planet and teaching in your own time. However, in all cases, these things relate more to the scientific nature of man's expression and being on the particular planet at which he is at the present time living.

Thus, in the city below, you will find hundreds, yes even thousands of places where mankind, in all levels of life, is learning a new and better way. We might say that these Centers express themselves in the field of biochemistry or with the various organic substances which enter into the bodies in these earth-life expressions or they may be mechanical inventions and contrivances. They may also relate to the more physical field of medicine, where are taught such things as drugs and various processes for healing the human body by the more commonly known physical aspect. While in a pure sense physical healing should be related to mankind from his higher self, yet such forms of physical healing on your earth plane are very necessary and vital for your present stage of evolution. Thus it is that you must set a broken bone and tape it up with splints, but there have been others on your earth at different times and even some in your modern day who could heal these bones by the thought projections of the radiant energies. So will you and others like you, in your evolution through what you call time and space, learn of the proper usage of the radiant energies and in your relationship to these energies, you shall be able to correct those conditions as they arrive.

Some of these spiritual healers who have appeared on your earth plane have been known as the Kuhuna or the fire-walkers or priests of the ancient origin, who knew of the various practices which completely separated man from his lower physical nature and enabled him to walk upon fire or to heal broken bones and other organic disturbances. So it was with the Master Jesus upon the earth plane and with many others who have appeared from time to time. I might say of your present medical science, that while there are many doctors who are practicing medicine on your earth plane and are somewhat intuitively aware of the God-Force from the infinite nature of man, yet they are too traditionally steeped in the practices of the test tube and the scalpel to fully recognize the God-Force which heals all people, irrespective of the nature of treatment or operation which was performed upon the body. So in the end, the earth doctor will, in his evolution, learn to discard such implements and will learn the true nature of science and the healing therapy as it is expressed from the inner nature of man's being.

Let us now descend the mountain and enter into this great city which you see stretched before you. As we approach one of the main entrances which appear from time to time upon the outer rim, we will see that it is glowing with a strange iridescent color. While at first it appears to be white, now you see that it is glowing almost like a rainbow. This is because the radiant energies which compose these buildings in their crystalline structure are of the radiant energy nature which stems from the Central Vortex, or as it has been called, from Venus, the Fountainhead.

It has suddenly occurred to me that I have not allowed you sufficient time to look about and properly evaluate the things which you have seen about you. So before we enter the city of Parhelion, let us look back and review somewhat what we have seen. Looking back up the mountain from where we were, you will see that we have descended through what looks like an earth pine forest. You may be somewhat surprised to see the likeness of the more familiar coniferous trees which abound on the mountain slopes of your native planet. However, here the difference is quite apparent, as they too, like all of the things about you seem to be glowing with a particular sparkling brilliance. There are also what appears to be streams of pure crystal-like water, tumbling down from over the rocks. Overhead the sky is filled with great cloudy masses of rainbow-hued colors. They are not like the clouds of your earth planet but are the actual radiant energies which fill space. These cloud formations of energies very often fall as a mist or rain which is collected on the mountains and flows into the streams, just as it does on your earth planet. If you will pause and think for a moment, you will see that the rain which falls on the earth, though it comes from a great cloud-like mass, yet it is essentially a form of energy, inasmuch as it turns the wheels of the dynamo which furnishes the power to run your great cities.

In the case here, as in the other planes of Shamballa, a much more highly evolved state of energy transmission is entered into. Therefore, as it was previously explained, the forests and the trees of your lower earth planets are first manifest in the spiritual planes. They are counterparts or spiritual natures of the trees as they appear in the lower planes. You will notice too, that there is some difference as to the coloration and the general appearance or feel of the things about you compared to what was on Venus. This is, of course, due to the relative nature of the plane in which we express ourselves, or from which we live and is somewhat different than on Venus. You will notice also that you are walking on a particularly brilliant shade of green grass that feels much like a deep soft carpet to your feet; this grass seems to sparkle like a million jewel-like emeralds.

Before we enter the building, we will enter a path which, instead of the more familiar drab or gray stone-like surfaces with which you are familiar, will also be of a rainbow-like beautiful substance. The city which you saw from the mountain top would be worthy of a little more adequate description as it was generally summarized as a wheel-like city with a large center hub with seven radial spokes, all extending out into and through a rather thick rim. Each of these seven spokes, in emerging from this rim, form an entrance into what you might call a dimension or plane, inasmuch as the various other planes, which are connected in the Shamballa, all use the separate entrances respective to the dimension from whence the persons come. Such things are, of course, necessary because of the nature of vibration and energy in which they work.

Around and about the city are great areas which are devoted to a particularly beautiful type of landscaping. While on Venus much of the city and of the landscaping was of a more, shall I say, less formal nature, here everything is laid out with the utmost precision in geometrical patterns, all expressing some idea or form of the science which is being expressed from this planet. You will see great trees and hedges, beautiful flower beds, all formed and sculptured with the utmost precision. The flowers themselves, are wonders of beauty. This one in particular, as you stoop over and seem to touch it, looks like a flame of glowing red color, where actually it is a rose and very similar to one on your earth plane, except that here too it is expressing a spiritual counterpart. And so you might walk for many days through the parkways which surround this vast city and see wonders and beauty which defy description and are beyond the imagination. Towering cypress trees are sculptured into various forms and seem to pierce the very heavens. Other and numerous groups, types and varieties of trees are in profusion and in abundance. There are also the familiar forms of lakes or small bodies of water which you would naturally associate with this type of landscaping. Here too, is an expression of life found in your lower earth plane orders. Just as in Venus, you will find forms of your various types of bird life and water-fowl in abundance all, in themselves, expressing their own higher state of evolution.

You will notice that we do not have sunshine here in terms of what you might call sunshine on your earth plane. As the sun here is in a more normal relationship than the earth's sun, there is not such a sharp contrast; therefore, the sun does not assume a personal brilliancy or a focal point of light. Instead, it is infused with the radiant energies which form from the heavens above you. As you can see by looking upward, there are great masses of energy that seem to form clouds. These are in a number and variety of colors; the blue, purple, gold, pink, and red shades are in abundance, and in a way they are somewhat reminiscent of your more familiar earth clouds. They will, in turn, sometimes form or precipitate themselves in energy streams of rain from the mountain tops.

The city which you see before you, now that you are closer to it, assumes a much different proportion than it did on the mountain top. Actually this city covers several hundred square miles in circumference, and there are not one but many floors or levels in the crystal-like structures. The city is divided into very definite sections or planes wherein the persons of different levels of evolution from the other planetary structures can enter into somewhat of a clairvoyant or suspended state and thus be taught. It might be well and interesting for your earth scientists to know that many of the scientists who formerly lived on your earth are here in this city of Parhelion. Such men as Galileo, Archimedes, Plato, Pythagoras, Einstein, Sir Isaac Newton, and a host of others who have at different times expressed something of a scientific relationship with your earth plane have been in this city at different times.

As on Venus, there are other cities which we can say are something of the substructures which relate to the lower or elemental type of science; here however, we are expressing a more pure and esoterical or spiritual science in regard to the lower orders of the earth planes. And while we do teach in the various laboratories things of an electronic or even a more material nature, yet there is an overall plan wherein the student is participating in such an active part as it would engage a futuristic plan. Such a program was entered into with the man called Jesus; and while He did not actually go into some of the materialistic aspects of science, as it is expressed on your present-day earth plane, yet He did go through the various necessary degrees on this planet which enabled Him to obtain a very conclusive and constructive relationship with mass, energy and of all things pertaining to an understanding. Not only did He become acquainted with all of these things, but so set Himself up in a plan whereby He was able to demonstrate the spiritual side of life to the earth people. Science can be expressed in two ways: in a material sense or in a spiritual sense. It is thus that man on this plane is learning the difference between the material and the spiritual science. With his twentieth-century day, electrical mechanisms and motivations, he will learn that these are primarily motivated by his sense of material values. In other words, he has not yet ascended into his mental scale of evolution whereby these things will be superseded by a much more intelligent approach and evaluation to his true position in God's great Celestial universe.

In the evolutions of time man will put aside the various and sundry equations which he has materialized into his physical world and they will, in turn, be superseded by a new science which deals with the spiritual nature of energy. So the scientist of your present world is due for many surprises and many shocks in his evolution, unless, of course, he evolves into these things in a more lengthy and natural sequence. Presenting these things to him at this time as a verbatim description will, I believe, defy the utmost length and confines of his imagination. He will be unable to perceive much of what will be given in this and other books, but do not be troubled for we here know factually and without error that these things do exist in much higher states of consciousness than man on your earth plane has ever dreamed of. It is our purpose to put aside the preconceived and well-defined conventional lines in which man has lived for many hundreds of years on your earth plane. It is the time of the new awakening, the time in which the spiritual values must be brought into man's consciousness; otherwise he shall surely perish, because he has completely over-balanced his world with a preponderance of a false material superstructure which will come crashing down upon him, unless he so properly constructs his life that it will be a more substantial and a more worthwhile world to live in.

Our future exploration of the city of Parhelion will be necessarily, and for obvious reasons, confined purely to the aspects of teaching. Because of the mental obstructions of the earth people, we will not attempt, at this time, to give any dialogues or dissertations from individuals or from former inhabitants of your earth plane. These things are, in themselves, relative and mean something which may be, at the moment, very pertinent or vital only to the person who is so exploring the scientific reaches of God's Infinite Nature. Our purpose here is more thoroughly defined, but until a little further along may I close this particular transmission and wish you all, for the moment, the most gracious and abundance of God's love.

CHAPTER 32

Do not feel surprised at seeing someone here before you who is different than your former guide Nikola. I am he who you once called Leonardo da Vinci on your earth planet. It is only fitting in a case of this kind that we should welcome you with the utmost hospitality and with the highest reception committee which is possible for us to muster up—no less than the best here for you. I see that you are looking at me and wondering just a bit about some of the things of my clothing and so on.

Yes, it is understandable that you are a little excited and may I say that we here, are also somewhat excited. We have long looked forward to the day when we here on Eros could come to your earth plane in a fuller concept and understanding. While there have been a few there who have occasionally glimpsed or surmised that we were in existence, still nothing definite or informative has yet been given. As it was said before, there is a proper time and place for everything. I would, however, like to clear up a few points which heretofore have been somewhat neglected. Nikola explained that our orbit was somewhat of an elongated ellipse or ellipsoidal orbit which took about 3800 years to complete. In this rather elongated ellipse, your earth planet is exactly in the center of the passing and the coming. In other words you could take an elastic band between two fingers and in stretching it out, place a marble half-way in between.

That would give you something of a rough picture of how your earth fits into our orbit. (It must be borne in mind that this is an abstract equation which is comparable to a tuning in and out process, something similar to a television or radio transmission.) Thus it is that every nineteen hundred years, we come into a comparatively close proximity with your earth planet. I might also say that this planet is about three times the size of the earth or Venus; it has no rotation or axis inclination as there is no need for such. Unlike Venus it possesses no atmosphere whatsoever. Venus has a rather spiritual or elevated type of atmosphere condition in which the various constituents of oxygen and the rare gases have been in somewhat of an evolved condition. However, in our case there is no atmospheric envelope nor is there any ionosphere. We are therefore in contact at all times with the outside dimension which you call space; and as you look up into the heavens above, you can see there the full impact of that meaning, as even the air about you seems to be filled with some sort of a pulsating radiant quality.

But come, let us walk down this pathway through the parkway toward one of the larger entrances. As you saw from the mountain top, our city is constructed in a heliocentric manner and the large central hub or axis, as you will see, will be the gathering place or the central temple. It will be also the place where the ascensions take place into the other realms and dimensions. Now I might explain some of the functions and relative values of our service in this city. As we are the fifth of the seven cities of the Shamballa, as you earth people call it, we are very functional in the respect that our work relates primarily to scientific aspects, yet is it not so that there is some science in everything which man does? An artist will use science in the mixture of his paints as well as in the application; likewise the musician, in the composition of his notes, combines basic harmonic frequencies. So in all expression you will find a very definite relative value of science in whatever expression of creativeness which man does. So therefore our planet and the city of Parhelion in particular form a vital and particularly integrated service which relates to, not only teaching but to learning the various scientific aspects of all of these creative sciences, whether it be medicine, art, literature, leadership, or any specific thing which you might care to name. It is therefore that we have constructed this city with seven entrances; each entrance is used by its own respective planet or the portion of Shamballa and their respective peoples. As all frequencies in their basic structures between these various seven planes are somewhat different in their relationship, it is necessary that the person who comes into this city be somewhat changed in frequency so that he can function more properly. It is not exactly a clairvoyant state but it does mean basic fundamental frequency changes. Therefore, you will see at the entrance of each of the seven great doorways, there is a certain device which helps focus certain energy beams into the persons who are passing through, thus they are automatically energized and conditioned for their stay in our city, in whatever capacity of learning or in whatever particular portion of the city they may take their studies or do their teaching.

On the planet Venus, the structures in the domed ceilings were carefully explained to you as performing certain functions which were relative to focusing energies so that they could properly reinforce the mind energies which were likewise being used in conjunction. The mind energies in that case were catalytic in nature and helped to perform and shape into an intelligent, cohesive and adhesive relationship, that particular thing in which the person or persons were thus constructing for themselves, as you saw in the birth of our sister Orda. Likewise such functions are performed, shall I say, in a reverse manner, as in the ascension. These things are likewise done on this and on the other remaining centers of Shamballa. However, in our science here, we do not have the obstructing, atmospheric, gaseous layer or the somewhat extended ionosphere; therefore our science relates to a slightly different concept.

As you will see, there is much in the way of prismatic arrangements in which giant prisms separate the various bands or frequency spectra, and thus focus them or so arrange them that they form certain cohesive relationships. These bands or streams of energy are thus directed with our minds in such shape or form and pattern as best suits our needs. You will also see that there are centers which are devoted to the more materialistic phases in man's learning on the lower earth planes. You may actually see in some of the classrooms certain students beginning to understand some of the fundamental relationships of such things as electric motors, vacuum tubes, and other paraphernalia which the earth man has found necessary in his evolution in science. Such things, of course, will be taught and learned in other earth life planes of existence throughout the universe, as your earth plane is one of many thousands which have a certain plus or minus relative value of materiality.

Now I believe I will describe something of my own personal past as it is similar to most of us here on Eros. As you see, I resemble the Venuseans except that I am about six or seven inches taller in height and more slender. Also I seem to be of an intense white radiance rather than of the yellow radiance which was characteristic of the Venuseans. However, as you see, I am wearing a loose fitted tunic which drapes over my shoulders and falls down below my knees. This tunic is composed of very finely woven, radiant energies, and appears to be rather translucent so that you are able to see my body shining through. I am, of course, using the term, earth-body loosely when compared with your material earth bodies as there is nothing material in your sense of the word, about my body. You can also see, if your eyes are accustomed to the brilliance, the certain radiant energy centers which have been previously described to you as existing in the feet, the solar plexus, the forehead and at the various points of the spine, as well as the fingertips and the centers of the palms. In other words, I may appear—if I can use something in comparison with your everyday earth life—like some of the neon signs which light up your streets.

However, I will not try to tempt you with humor at this present moment. Our mission is far too sacred and grave to indulge in frivolities, presently. Now we have passed down the pathway until we are standing before this very large doorway—actually it is not a doorway but merely an entrance. As we are about to enter in, you will see over the archway, which is about some 25 or 30 feet high, that there is a certain symbol. This is the symbol which denotes the planet or the center from which the various peoples come. In this case it is the symbol of the planet Venus. As you were just in contact with this planet, it was thought your vibrations would be more conducive and less confusing at this moment. There is also another reason as you will soon find out when we pass through this portal. Now as we are going through you will notice that there is a circular ring of prisms of intense radiant colors through which you will directly pass. While they may have no effect upon you because you have been preconditioned and are in a different state of consciousness, yet they do have a definite effect upon any person, especially from the planet Venus inasmuch as he will be somewhat conditioned after passing through this ring of prismatic colors. He will, in other words, be greatly tempered and conditioned for whatever time he remains within the city. Now that we have come down the hallway, we will first turn into one of the larger rooms. However, before we fully examine this room, I believe that a little more definite description of this great center would be of value to you here. The various spokes, of which there are seven, are divided within the central section of the outer rim into seven sections, just as you would cut a pie. In this case, the slice would be exactly between the ends of the spokes; each section there, however, will represent to some degree, the limits of the particular type of teaching or learning which is in progress at the moment. There are, of course, other things besides teaching and learning, such as museums, places of convalescence, places of rest and meditation and other points of interest which are necessary. In the center of these spoke-like sections, there are more landscaped gardens and parkways with lakes where the various persons come at different times and wander through in states of contemplation or meditation.

Now that we are about to go into this large room, I might say here is a part of the previous book which was not given to you from the planet Venus, and for obvious reasons, because it was necessarily a function performed in conjunction with the planet Venus. That is the part which relates to people who have become mentally disarranged and with various mental aberrations of such nature that it is necessary to have certain special types of treatment before the proper rest and convalescence, and spiritual therapy is applied. This is done through various scientific apparatus of a very highly evolved nature of which the earth planet scientist would know little or nothing about. I believe in your past few years of experience, you have had some inkling of the nature of these types of apparatus and of the nature of the things which they can do.

I will attempt too, before we are through with this ward, to go somewhat into the relative values of a science which has at different times been practiced, rather closely or loosely on your earth planet—the problem of casting out evil adherences or, as it has been called, exorcism. The man Jesus was well versed in this science; in fact, he took much of his training in this very ward. The casting out of evil spirits is a science which would be of great advantage for the earth psychiatrist to learn. Many of the people who are incarcerated in the various mental institutions would be almost instantaneously liberated could such proper mental therapy be applied. I say to the scientist on the earth who is confining his therapies to the mind, that there is no condition or aberration, whatever you may call such a condition, which is not someway, directly or indirectly, related to such possessive mental adherences which are called obsessions. There are, in the lower orders of spiritual existences, such types of distorted mental phenomena which pass all beliefs. Some of the descriptions of these things have been rather loosely called demons or devils and ogres. It is the type of mentality which has been switched from the constructive and the supernormal into the subnormal reaches which you call the subastral plane.

The earth scientist, at your present time, has little use for such beliefs in spite of the great work which was done by the great Avatar Jesus. The New Testament as well as other portions of your Bible, not to mention many pages of historical evidence, support the entire truth of this wonderful and badly neglected science on your earth plane. It is one of the phases of spiritual progression in which the earthman will have to re-enter and re-learn before he attains his peaceful state of evolution.

Now let us pass through the doorway into this large ward. As you see, it is somewhat like the ones you saw on Venus, and there are, stretching out into a long distance away, vast numbers and rows of cot-like beds in which people seem to be sleeping. This ward is devoted primarily to a more convalescent type of therapy after the mental adhesions have been removed, as it has been called in your Bible, "to cast out the devils". If you so desire, although I do not recommend it, you may visit and even go with some of us into the lower realms where we remove, at different times, some of these cases of mentally obsessed people who are passing from the various mental institutions of your country. However, I may say that such an experience would not be pleasant and I would not recommend it unless you think you are thoroughly fortified, as it may leave you in a very completely muddled state of mind.

We will stroll about a few moments and as you see, there are people of all types and all ages here; people who have broken down under the various pressures of the different ways of the civilized world, people who have broken down through fear and ignorance and of the various psychosomatic neuroses which were incurred through mistreatment and malpractice in their infancy. Some of these people brought over their mental conditions from a previous evolution and relived them again on your earth plane. It is needless to say they were thoroughly misunderstood and badly abused and little if anything was done for them. And so it is up to us and, with the help and consciousness of their relatives and friends and those who are in spiritual work to project positive thoughts for them, these energies are so used. They are the catalytic agents to use the supreme energy of the God-Force in directing the reconstruction of their badly warped and distorted psychic bodies. You know (speaking to the Moderator) something of the construction of the psychic body by now, so I will not attempt to go into any more detailed explanation.

You will notice that the color of many of these people present very peculiar conditions; for instance, here is one who seems to be a dull purplish-black color. This person was at one time a violently insane person and passed from an earth ward hospital in a straitjacket. There are other conditions; each one presents its own individual case and its own individual heart-breaking story, a bit of humanity which was tossed into a sea of materialism which had little understanding and much less pity for their condition. You are seeing one of these many wards of convalescence although I may say that they cover many acres of ground if I can put this in the dimensions of the earth terms. There are literally many thousands of these cases of the mental nature of people who have passed on in this condition, and which require this special type of therapy before they can be transferred to other places for further treatment. Mental conditions, especially those which are incurred through adhesions or obsessions as you more commonly termed the word, are particularly difficult to reconstruct because this takes place in a dimension and a plane which is unrelative to the place in which it was incurred. If a person on the earth plane could re-enact in similar conditions such a time and place in a psychic way that would be conducive to mental therapy, many of these cases could be, of course, instantaneously healed, as was in the case of the Master Jesus who went about, cast out and liberated many of the diseased or obsessed conditions; however, after a person passes from the plane in which these conditions were incurred, healing is very difficult because we do not have the voluntary cooperation of the patient. Likewise we do not have the intelligence or the cooperation of those who are more directly concerned and who revolve about him in his own native vibrations.

However, I do believe that you are becoming just a little bit tired with my rapid fire conversation; so I believe that for the time being we shall temporarily suspend our narration and our exploration. And may we send you a special ray of love.

Leonardo.

CHAPTER 33

Greetings to you again, brother and sister. Your earth scientist would be very surprised if he knew of the vast distance which he calls space and which you span in a split second of time that enables you to arrive here upon our planet and in our city. I see that we are standing again in the ward where we left off our previous transmission; but before resuming our discussion in psychiatry and obsession, let me say that your arrival here in this particular city was timed at such a moment that you would be able to witness at least a part of some of the ceremonies which were attendant to a conclave of various forces which came from the different planetary systems. These conclaves or gatherings are a part of the science which is taught here in Parhelion. However, this particular observance and ceremony does not start for a day or so and meanwhile, we will resume some of the more pertinent and vital issues which are expressed in this city. I believe that we were looking at some of the more convalescent cases which were ready for transportation to other planets. By now you will have rightly assumed that one of our functions here is that of a receiving hospital where many of the various types of insane and badly warped and distorted psychic bodies are brought to us for treatment. We also sometimes organize with the other members of the different planets, such as Venus, such organizations as are suitable to go into the lower reaches of the astral worlds and remove some of these obsessed cases which have been brought to our attention through the prayers and intercessions of their loved ones. However, in all cases, we must have some sort of intercession before such conclusions can be brought about and our attention focused on a particular case.

In the study and science of psychiatry, the earth scientists have only a small fraction of a portion of the things which relate to the particular state of consciousness of any individual who is under his care or observation. It has been explained in previous discussions from the book of Venus that such psychiatry takes place only in the immediate realm and dimension of the physical life of the individual which is at that moment on the earth plane. The reason for the large number of people who are incarcerated in your various asylums and penal institutions is the lack of thorough and complete knowledge of man's progression and evolution through the many stages of his development.

In classifying the various types of obsessions, we say that there are two definite and basic divisions: those obsessions which are self-inflicted and those which are incurred through wrong thinking or lack of proper constructive evaluation of the life principles. Negation is, of course, primarily responsible for all types of obsession. However, you may be surprised to know that a person can actually, through a strong pattern of a continual recurrence of negative ideas, form such a substance in a spiritual world around him that it will assume a thought form body which will badly warp and distort him. These are particularly difficult to remove, as they are actually a part of him and usually entail some sort of manipulative process which you might almost think something akin to some of the more surgical processes involved in the operating room in the hospital of the earth. However, in this case, the energy is electronic in nature and no instruments are used. Instead, we use different types of beams or light frequencies or various other types of energy to remove these obstructing wave-form vortexes from the psychic body. There are many such types of rooms where this type of therapy is applied for different cases. However, because of the vastness of this subject and of the limitations of time and space, not to mention such factors as the element of confusion which might enter into your mind, we will, by necessity, be forced to conclude something of these in more or less of a general summation of such conditions. To the earth person, may I say this: that his continual thinking, as he calls his active conscious thought process in the world about him, can be similarized to a radio sending and receiving set for he is in instantaneous attunement with all the creation about him, and that he also sends out wave forms which will attract or repel such like or unlike frequencies. It is much the same as the radio that sits upon your table, except in a much more expanded scale of consciousness. A moment's thought and reflection into this will immediately alert a person to the tremendous possibilities of the state-of-mind consciousness and that he automatically tunes himself in with planes of existence as they are relative to his particular thought processes at that particular moment.

Now, if it were not for some very important and vital factors, it is possible that most earth people would, in their continual recurrence of negation, completely destroy themselves or become obsessed in such manner that life would soon be impossible for them as they lack the more vital and constructive processes which are necessary for their daily life.

However, the all-wise and the almighty Father Intelligence which comes from the Central Vortex has anticipated such relative negations and, in fact, it was He who so inspired and built these planes of negative relationships so that you might be helped in generalizing your various multitude of aspects of life. Thus it has been, at your birth, that you have been surrounded, in a general sense of the word, with such relative forces which are necessary and conducive to a better way of life. These better forces are, of course, not impelling. They are simply subject to your will and dominion. In other words, as you so wish them, so they will desire. They stand by ready at all times to help, to aid, and to rectify such conditions to the utmost of their ability. They are, in other words, your guardian angels. Some of the spiritual concepts of the earth people call them the spirit band; however, this is more or less of a general term because it relates only to such people or forces who dwell in relative planes that are on the same constructive or the same vibratory plane of endeavor.

If you will think now, there are also other planes which are not so conducive to a general and a better way of life. These negative planes are what you call the astral worlds and are such for people who have not lived a completely positive life and who will—at some time in their spiritual evolution, because of the lack of fundamental knowledge and a cohesive and adhesive relationship to life—revolve into these lower dimensions. Sometimes, of course, these individuals or persons assume such a distorted personality as to defy description. They are born from the ranks of such people who have lived on your earth planes as murderers, thieves and various mental and physical prostitutes of all kinds. They have continually recurred or reincarnated into such lower planes of expression and thus strengthened their thought patterns of life to such a point where they become almost demoniac and as they have sometimes been called, devils and various other types of the very destructive under-astral plane personalities.

To your earth people, may I say that a single destructive thought such as hate, envy, jealousy or rage will immediately tune you in, as it were, (using the vernacular of the earth scientist), to thousands or perhaps even millions of these lower earth plane astral entities. Were it not for your protecting and guiding forces, you would almost immediately be overwhelmed. This, in a large sense, explains to you that sometimes as these protective forces do break down after the continual indulgences in negation, such a person may go about with a stream of hateful or vengeful thoughts flowing through his mind that his forces will eventually break down and a lurking entity may come in, project him from his own body, and use his body as an instrument of murder and destruction. You have read these accounts in your daily newspapers of a person seemingly committing some heinous crime in a blacked out condition, awaking to find the body before him.

The psychiatrist of today does not deal in these pertinent facts. He refuses to acknowledge the dominating factors which relate man to his life upon the earth plane. As I have said, it would be impossible for a person to sustain life upon this earth plane if it were not for the continual flow of energy into his body from the Central Infinite Vortex. This, I believe, has been explained to you in other writings and in other chapters, and I need not go to any length or dissertation to explain the processes whereby this energy flows into the body. It is an occurrence of misalignment of this ever-permeating force into your bodies which will cause other diseased conditions termed incurable, or which your earth doctor or scientist knows little or nothing about.

He is continually looking for these symptoms in the human body or the physical body and in which place they are not, and cannot be cured. So until the future day when the earth doctor becomes clairvoyant and able to peer into the past or the akashic record of the individual or patient under observation, he will have little or no success with these conditions, nor will it be that the high rate of incidence of insanity and various mental aberrations which are confined in your mental and penal institutions be lessened. In fact, as you know from statistics, the load is increasing and growing heavier every day. It is estimated that at least one person out of sixteen is badly in need of such mental treatment. The way of life on the earth planet at the present time is not conducive to any lengthy or enjoyable state of peace of mind.

There are thousands and innumerable compensations in your daily life which give rise to frustrations and eventually to neurotic conditions which have to be, in some way or in some form, adjusted. Your earth doctor or psychiatrist has only made a partial step forward in the proper evaluation of these psychiatric conditions. He may have instituted himself into such a position and that by using such nomenclature or terminology of words has constructed for himself a dimension or a world within your world which is a superimposed facility of knowledge and wisdom which he actually does not possess. I am not, in any sense of the word, chiding or mentally castigating any of the earth scientists at the present time. I am merely pointing out these things so that they may be interwoven into your future daily lives.

The patients who you see in the wards about you shall, in a few days' time, disappear into other worlds and into other places and they will be replaced by a continually emerging stream of these badly malformed wrecks from the astral worlds. And I may say that these are only a small fraction of those who are thus cared for in other portions of this great city. If we were to explore some of these other wards, you might be almost shocked beyond the point of sanity in viewing some of these badly malformed wrecks which have been brought to us; and so for this particular purpose and this time, I will not endeavor to show you any of them. However, I may say that some of the things which you find in your penal institutions on your earth plane are but mild in comparison to what their actual psychic bodies in their malformed conditions are when they arrive here on this side of life in their spiritual sense. They, in some way, defy description and as I have said, they would completely nauseate you to a point where you might be seriously affected mentally.

Now for the moment, I believe I have discussed sufficiently this question of psychiatry. There are still some rather pertinent points which I would like to bring up in what might be called the realm of astrophysics. In the opening chapters of your book of Venus, an allegorical equation was brought to your mind of a soap bubble in which it was pointed out that the universe was some such a structure, or could be pictured as such. Under a powerful magnifying glass, it was seen that there were tiny round-shaped particles which were adhering to each other through the law of adhesive relationship. If we extend this picture just a little further so that we can picture to the earth scientist or astrophysicist something of what he calls his universe, we will begin to blow up this bubble into such proportions that it would completely enclose your solar system. If you were to stand somewhere on the outside of this vast huge bubble and see your planets revolving inside, then you would begin to grasp something of the size. Now, under a microscope, you would see that the tiny particles had so expanded in size that they were no longer touching each other and that the spaces in between would be filled with some sort of a radiant energy. You would also begin to see that your own solar system, as you call this, would be but one of these tiny little specks. If we were to blow up the soap bubble a little further and if we could also enclose other soap bubbles within this soap bubble and then fill up the spaces also between these soap bubbles with radiant energy, we would begin to form some sort of a pattern of what the universe looks like.

Now, if we could so adjust the soap bubbles so that they would be continually, over periods of time, expanding and contracting within themselves so that the outermost would pass completely into the innermost and vice versa, then you would begin to grasp some sort of an idea of what the universe actually is. In the overall expanded condition of the soap bubble, your own greatest telescope and the utmost in its magnification would only picture some such small portion as might be covered by the smallest coin of your realm, such as a ten-cent piece. You can, therefore, assume from that, that your universe is much more than you have ever assumed it to be. However, I might point out that such a concept will only be properly evaluated through the process of time. It is, at the present moment, completely beyond your physical senses, nor should you attempt to evaluate these things properly. It is a mistake to assume any proportion of intelligence in relationship to the creative universe around you, until you have properly instituted yourself into such fundamental concepts which are more relative to your own plane of existence. In other words, we will begin at home first and clean our own house up before we can go over and clean up our neighbor's.

So in the future, to the earth scientist and to the astrophysicist and to the doctor, let us begin thoroughly to conquer the conditions of the earth plane. When we can say that war is no longer present in your planet, that you have also emptied your asylums and your prisons and your various other types of institutions wherein human wreckage is incarcerated, and that you have fully evolved into such a conscious state that such things can be cured in a properly related manner, then it will be the time for you to start exploring the outer realms of space; and in such a proper time and place, so shall you be given the knowledge and the proper wisdom for which to do so. Until that time, however, we will resume our narration at a later date.

CHAPTER 34

Greetings again, and I believe I have correctly anticipated your eagerness to resume our exploration of the city of Parhelion. Before we leave this large ward of healing, let us pause a moment and look back, so that you may have a better description in your mind to give to your earth brothers. As you see, it is somewhat reminiscent of the large healing wards which you saw on Venus. However, there are some differences. In the ceilings, instead of the parabolic reflectors or lenses, we see that there are prisms which are very large in size, usually about three to five feet from apex to apex. These prisms are constructed of crystallike material which have their own particular properties of separating various energy frequencies into streams or beams of pencil-like light which are reflected into the psychic bodies of the individuals resting upon their cots of energy masses. These particular frequency beams of energies are so relative in their dimension that they are all constructed for healing in their particular frequency and replace or regenerate and replant certain malformed vortexes within the psychic body.

Thus, these people, while they may appear to be sleeping and entirely without any particular movement of body or seemingly unintelligent in any way, are actually in a very dreamy state of consciousness. They may be reliving some of the past scenes of their previous lives. They may even be going through some of the experiences in a psychic way which related them to their particular condition at the moment. Thus it is that these things are rectified and reconditioned and new and radiant energies are implanted into the psychic bodies to replace those which have been badly distorted or malformed.

You will also note that passing about through the corridors, there are a number of my fellow Eroseans. These are, of course, distinguishable from all of the others. They are, in some sense, what might be called interns and some of them have been in and out of these wards for something like hundreds of your earth years. There are others, of course, from the planet Venus itself. I have pointed out that our service from this planet, while it is one primarily dedicated to science and occupies the fifth ray position, yet it also serves in conjunction with the other six centers of Shamballa in teaching and in learning and in the reconstructive processes in which the other six centers cannot function properly in that pure sense of science. As I have said, all of these facets or phases are relative and dependent upon each other, and are very strongly interwoven. I would like to say at this time too, that while our city of Parhelion appears to you very vast and very large, yet there are other cities upon this planet in the lower dimensions which also relate to some particular function or transmission of learning and teaching to other astral worlds and in other dimensions. Ours, of course, is in a sense related to the higher forces which you call the Shamballa.

Now I believe that while we are passing down the halls, we will enter into another room. This room, as you will see in stepping through, is a storage room. I am showing you this because of the great numbers of various types of electronic apparatus which is stored in this room and used from time to time by the various factions which are so schooled in its use. These are somewhat reminiscent of the large search-lights or the X-ray machines and various other types of electronic apparatus which are, at present, used on your earth plane; except, of course, here these instruments and electronic devices are all of a much more highly evolved nature, and their function is in realms which are, shall I say, supersonic or beyond the realm of any known earth-plane expression. Now that you have been gazing somewhat in wonder and awe about this great room and looking at some of these rather fearsome-looking pieces of electronic equipment, let us pass down the hall into what I will call an operating room.

While we are thus occupied, I shall explain to you that the apparatus which you saw is very often transported into the physical world, into the operating rooms, into the wards, and into the homes and sick rooms of some of the earth planets just as your own, in cases where special types of therapy is to be applied and in which such rates of vibration or in which such barriers of time and space can be set aside temporarily so that the healing processes can be instigated. You must not assume for one moment that the pure power of prayer, as you call this, is the entire ingredient which is necessary in the healing process. While we may say, in the overall sense, it is the power of God and the Supreme Power which heals, yet it must be administered into its proper relationship and into its proper dimension. As God is infinite in nature, He manifests in an infinite number of concepts and dimensions, so that man in his various evolutions learns the proper administration of this particular concept. You eartheans must never feel alone in the hour of need for your thought conscious-

236

ness, if it is properly projected as you call this prayer, will be intercepted and used either by us or some relative plane which is close to your existence.

Now we are emerging into this great, shall I say, operating room. As I said before, we do not use knives or scalpels, nor do we seemingly tear a physical body apart. However, we will approach the area in the center of the room where you see a large group of people who are standing around what appears to you to be a rather enlarged version of an operating table. Now that we are in easy eyesight of this procedure, you will see that there is rather a strange-looking object lying on the table. Overhead you will notice that there is a whole battery of prismatic lights which are reflecting a rather strange and dancing light onto this object below. Around and about this table are also grouped some rather strange-looking pieces of apparatus which are gleaming and shining and seem to reflect an innumerable number of very strange-looking contrivances. These things, in themselves, defy description. I will not attempt at this time to try to put these things into earth words.

I believe you saw something of a similar condition in a laboratory on the planet Mars, however, you will agree with me that this particular thing supersedes and far out-weighs anything which you may have previously witnessed. You will see also that there are two of my fellow Eroseans who seem to be manipulating various electrodes or devices upon this object which is lying on the table.

Now, let us get a little closer and see just what this object is. At first you may think it looks like some strangely distorted body. Actually it is two bodies. To point out this particular case, may I say that the operation taking place here is the separation of

two human beings in their psychic forms. It began
with a story of a mother on the earth planet many,
many years ago who died from a cancer. During the
period before she passed from the earth plane, she
became tremendously obsessed with the consciousness of the cancer, and in building up this tremendous fear within herself, she constructed a thought
form body which became very firmly enmeshed and
entwined in her own psychic body. In passing over
into the spiritual world, this body could not be
separated from her by her relatives or friends, and in
the confusion which followed, she in her fear and
panic attached herself firmly into the psychic body
of her daughter.

Later on, her daughter became obsessed with the
fear of cancer to such a point that the cancer was re-
inflicted into the physical body of the daughter. At the
point where she visited the physician to test whether
the lump in her breast was a malignant cancer, she
had not been at any time forewarned of this condition. The physician assured her that it was cancer
and that an operation was necessary. In the following
wave of panic and fear, the woman climbed out of a
ten-story building and precipitated herself into the
street below.

Now these doctors here are attempting to separate the mother and the daughter. When they have
done so they will have to separate the thought form
bodies of the gray masses which you see and which
are interwoven and intertwined by tiny thread-like
strings which seem to flow into the psychic bodies of
the individuals. This is a very laborious and indeed a
delicate process to do. When these things have finally
been separated, you will find just as you saw on the
planet Venus and in their particular convalescing
wards that all that remains of the daughter's suicide

body is something which will have to remain in more or less of a suspended state until such proper healing therapies can be administered which will enable her to reenact her earth-plane existence. As for the mother, she too will have to be conditioned at some other place and some other time. She, too, will have to have the vortexes of fear thoroughly and completely removed and cleansed from her psychic body. She too will have to learn to grasp the infinities of God's nature, and thus she will inure, into herself, the idea that life is perpetual and that the continuity of life is perpetual and that all we have to fear is the fear of ourselves.

As you have correctly surmised, we have related each definite segment of the city of Parhelion to its own particular office and function on one of the other planes of Shamballa. While we have, in ourselves, one of these sections which functions in the realm of pure science, we do not feel, however, at this time that it would be wise for you to investigate the other remaining sections of this city until you have been given a somewhat similar book as to the book of Venus in its particular relative field of science or spiritual leadership or of the arts or of the other particular relative dimensions in which this city expresses itself.

As I previously mentioned in another transmission, we are about to observe something of a ceremony which we have been conducting for the past several years in the relationship of your earth planet. You must know that your earth planet is like many other planets at this particular time tied up in, shall I say, a state of time or evolution which is very pertinent and vital to the welfare of the inhabitants. It has so been contrived and conceived in the divine mind of God that the various planets and the peoples who dwell therein must evolve into different relative states of consciousness. Thus they assume a proper proportion of balance in their viewing or their aspects of life. Your own earth plane is passing through one of these stages at the present moment. Thus it is that we here on Eros, as well as on the other six centers of the Shamballa, convene at regular monthly intervals (if I can put the time quotient into this) for the purposes of projecting a particularly strong ray or beam into the earth mind consciousness of all the peoples on the earth planes.

While these rays are not, in themselves, felt or physically ascertained into any individual's particular physical mind or is his consciousness so disturbed that he may feel or manifest a consciousness of such wave, nevertheless, these energies are, shall I say, shone into his psychic body so that he will in the days following find a renewed strength and courage. He will also find a new sense of spiritual values. These rays are being directed particularly to the leaders of the two great nations of the earth. It is, I believe, part of the result of projecting these rays that you have found a renewed concentrated effort in the political fields in regard to your neighbors across the seas. We are in a sense using something of a broadcasting system which is done at certain intervals of time for the purpose of swinging the balance or the preponderance of weight against the great masses of negative force which are seeking to overwhelm your planet.

And so it is that we will step down the hall into the central temple, if I may call it such, where we may witness the first of the series of these projection sessions. As we enter this vast hall, we will see that it is far larger than any of your earth plane stadiums where you conduct the athletic carnivals. It might be said that it can seat approximately a half million souls. Now that we have stepped inside this huge great theater of our temple, we will take a seat here which is close by the corridor and we can watch the proceedings. As you will see, it is laid out in a circular fashion similar to the smaller Venusian temple in the city of Azure, and that it is also constructed of the intense white crystalline substances which are similar to that temple. However, there are some other distinguishing factors. Besides the tremendous size of this auditorium or temple is the ceiling itself. You will notice that around the central part of the ceiling is a huge circle wherein are placed a large number of giant prisms of light. Now that we are seated, you will see that as the temple is already filled, there are certain segments within this circle which are slowly withdrawing, something in sections similar to how you would peel or section an orange. These sections are sliding down into the roof below, leaving a large exposed circular area in which the radiant energies of heaven seem to be streaming. Immediately below this on the floor is a huge raised block of pure crystal which is about one hundred feet square each way. Around on the four corners of this crystal are arranged four different projectors, if I may call them such. They are a very highly evolved type of an electronic apparatus which I will not attempt to describe. However, may I say that they are ray projection machines which will help intensify the energies of mind which are projected into the center area of these four dimensions.

Now as it was on the planet Venus and in the temple of Azure, we will slowly hear the sing-song rhythm of the energies which they are beginning to manifest and build up. You earth people, who are accustomed to the blaring of horns and to the strident noises of the voice and speech, will be somewhat disappointed as our ceremonies are simple and complete. We do not indulge in any frills or in any of the stage effects which are necessary to impress the earth people in the form of entertainment. Ours is purely a ceremony which is conducted and conducive to one purpose—to the projection of an intense ray of energy toward the earth. I might say here too that we have learned to turn our world upon its axis and thus we can turn it about and project it into such a way that it will shine directly onto the planet earth. We can also, at different times, so change the path or orbit of our planet Eros that it may seem to appear or disappear at different points of its original orbit. To you earth minds who have been so long steeped in the concept of time and space, this will be a little difficult to assimilate. However, it is truly so.

Now we will listen to the sing-song chant of the energies as they are building up. You will begin to see that there are great waves of energy which seem to be rolling toward the central platform of crystal. There they seem to be arranging and rearranging themselves into an innumerable number of tiny pinpoints and vortexes of light which seem to sparkle and cascade like a great brilliant fountain of energy in the center of this block of crystal. The four projectors are also by now in operation and they too are projecting an intense concentration of energies into this central area.

Now the fountain of energy rises higher and higher. It begins to form a long pencil-like streamer toward the central roof section which has been removed. Higher and higher streams this great pencil-like energy; then suddenly, in a great terrific burst, it seems to project in a long pencil-like beam outward, onward into space. At this moment, the crescendo of sound has reached an almost ear-splitting intensity, if I can use the word, earsplitting. However, these are merely vibrations which are superimposed in your consciousness and not from the physical sense of the ear. It merely means that your whole psychic body is palpitating with these radiant energies. This pencil-like beam will endure for possibly the space of time of about fifteen minutes of your earth time. However, we shall not remain for the sake of brevity until these things have been completed as I believe, also, that your psychic body might suffer from an over-exposure of the tremendous intensities of these rays. I see also that what you are calling your psychic vision or sight is somewhat blinded and blurred by the intensity of these rays.

This pencil-like beam, of course, will not be visible to your earth people since they are not attuned to the frequencies which are impinged within this beam. They are all, however, very wonderfully constructed energies which will recharge and revitalize the spiritual consciousness of your earth people. They will, of course, particularly appeal to those who are in the positions of scientific and political leadership.

So now, let us rest awhile. We will not wait until the energies die away for the termination of this visit. And so, may you rest until such further narration.

Rays of love to you again from Eros and from the city of Parhelion. I believe we were interrupted or discontinued our transmission shortly after the conclusion of the initial ceremony which opened the conclave of the seven cities of Shamballa. The purpose of this conclave which has brought many hundreds of thousands from the various centers throughout Shamballa is one of deep religious and spiritual significance. It also has a two-fold purpose, inasmuch as a new leader of the entire seven cities of Shamballa is about to be properly instituted in his office. A few days ago, you witnessed a ceremony of emergence of one of the Venusians who had been Lord and Master of Venus for two thousand years. He and his beloved biune mate took their departure from that planet and have now been awaiting this ceremony. As you have been told in this previous narration that this man formerly appeared on your earth plane two thousand years ago as the man called Jesus. He is now to be duly instituted into his new office and duties as Lord and Headmaster and Avatar of the seven Shamballas.

These ceremonies are necessarily sacred and they are also of a very highly evolved nature. We do not like to use the word secret. However, I believe it would be of the best interest to all those who read the book and these narrations that this particular initiation should largely be kept secret as many of the various ceremonies are of a very highly and very secret nature. However, that is still to come about in the future hours, so for the present let us resume somewhere where we left off. One reason why you were suddenly taken from the large central temple was because the tremendous power which was being manifest was severely shaking the various centers in your astral body. If such energy transference had continued, you might have been severely injured. Now, however, you are thoroughly safe and in a position whereby we continue our explorations of this segment of Parhelion.

I will open first by giving somewhat of a dissertation which is particularly directed to the earth scientists and doctors who are laboring in the fields which are associated with what he calls virus conditions. If he is open-minded, I believe that some of the transcript here would be of tremendous aid to him in conquering these seemingly unconquerable diseases. While the earth scientist or doctor knows these things exist, yet he is at a loss to explain their origin or how they multiply or recur in the human body. First, let us thoroughly and completely understand that these tiny sub-microscopic particles are purely the generic by products of your vastly complicated civilized age. You must realize that the mind processes which are continually being generated in the human mind in your civilized world are largely products of reactionaryism and very negative in nature. Because a person thinks a thought and discontinues that particular thought for something else, this does not mean that the thought has perished. Mind energy must and always does remain a part of the person from whence it was generated. This energy is also spontaneous in a certain sense, inasmuch as it relates itself in the law of harmonic relationship with all other such energies so generated. Thus the sum and total of all such continued and repeated generations of such energy, among the millions and millions of people who inhabit your earth plane, give rise to great seas of negative energies. These great seas or tides of negative energies hover around in the close proximity of the earth plane, something like the familiar morning ground fog that you are observant of when you arise early in the morning. However, in this case these negative energy fogs are invisible to your eyes. Nevertheless, they so exist.

Now, it is the nature of any of such generic energy that it possesses, in itself, a latent intelligence, if we can use the word intelligence loosely; whether it is constructively-minded or destructively-minded, it is still intelligence. Such energies as they are negative will not and cannot be denied unto themselves and so they must revolve around and around until they form tiny submicroscopic vortexes or hard nuclei of energy. They, therefore, manifest into such levels of subconsciousness with the individual who becomes slightly hypersensitive at the particular moment because of some dominant negative happening in his or her life. Children are particularly susceptible to such nuclei of energy which you call viruses. Thus it is, many of these nuclei or viruses enter into the nervous system of the child and polio is produced or perhaps it may be whooping cough or mumps or some of the other similar so-called virus conditions. These, in themselves, are purely the nuclei which you call viruses of negative thought forms or frequencies which are being continually generated in the minds of the people in the world today.

Proper therapy in the future will stem from such proper measures as will regulate the thinking of people into more productive and more useful and less reactionary thought patterns. Also, it will give rise to such machinery or such other types of instrumentation of electronic nature which can and does thoroughly dissipate or neutralize such negative nuclei which you call the viruses. These viruses, in themselves, are somewhat similar to the negative energies which cause cancer and some of the other incurable conditions throughout the body. Inasmuch as several of these nuclei, being intelligent, will, in a sense of the word, superimpose their intelligence into other atomic structures which are of a more productive intelligence, they will thus instill their destructive intelligence in the surrounding atomic structures and render them also unproductive and unintelligent. So this is a vicious treadmill chain-like fashion which spreads in a rapid form and through tiny threads throughout the human system. This you have called cancer or you may perhaps call it polio but remember, whatever particular conditions which you may call these things, they are very closely related and all stem from the same fields of negative thinking.

Now that we have somewhat covered the subject of viruses, cancer and some of the other conditions, I believe it is time for us to move on into another portion of the great city of Parhelion. Thus we will remove ourselves into a quarter which is related to our own particular aspects of the function of this planet. As I summarized before, there are six other different sections which are devoted and related to the functions of the other centers of Shamballa but here we, in ourselves, function independently alone in the fields of pure science. Now as we have come through a large doorway which links us with another of the radial spokes which stem from the great center temple, we will walk slowly up the central corridor which is something like about three hundred feet wide. On each side and up through the center are great cases which are filled on either side and both sides and along in the middle with innumerable and countless inventions which have existed in the world of your earth plane as well as in innumerable other earth planes. There are countless thousands of these inventions some of which you may recognize as the more crude implementation of the savages who inhabited your planet hundreds of thousands of years ago—such things as flint-headed arrows and clubs or stone-headed axes, clear up until your present-day age wherein you will see some of the types of the more modern weapons. There are also innumerable other inventions which relate to your earth plane— some of the more useful types. You will find every-thing from the safety pin, the egg beater and so on, are displayed here in one or some of the other cases.

It would probably take you several years to thor-oughly and completely cover this one corridor alone, as it relates not only to your earth plane but, as I have said, to countless other planetary systems which are located throughout the galaxy or star cluster which is somewhat covered by the activities of the planet Eros.

Now that we have somewhat skimpily gone through this great central corridor, we will finally arrive at the other end. Here you will see stretched out on either side of the periphery or the rim or great wheel are huge laboratories. In strolling through these great laboratories, you will find students and interns who come from all nations not only of the earth plane but from many other planets in the various solar systems with which we are associated. There will be all races, all colors and all creeds.

Some of these scientists are laboring and will produce inventions which are related to their own particular present day and age. Others here have been laboring to produce and to envision inventions which will relate you and the destinies of other planets into the many hundreds of years of your future life. It is quite obvious that here again we would be completely at a loss for time and that it would also take many, many years to go through these laboratories and make ourselves acquainted with even the more superficial aspects of these tremendous activities. However, it is my intention in the future, that as we cover the other remaining sections of Shamballa and that as you visit these various centers in their respective planets, that you will have a fitting addendum to each book which will relate the activities of that particular center to our own scientific work here. Thus it is that you will not only cover our particular scientific center a little more thoroughly, but you shall also cover the other remaining five segments.

It has been decided that while we were talking and continuing our exploration that you should witness the emergence of the new ruler of Shamballa.

This particular part of the ceremony will be shown to you, and you will witness this emergence in the full sacredness of the rite for which it is intended. I may inform you that this happens perhaps once every two thousand years or perhaps even at a longer time. The sacredness of this ceremony cannot be over-emphasized, inasmuch as all seven of the centers of Shamballa pledged themselves to the service of the great immortal Father and rededicate their lives in the complete fullness of such service. This they do in the full acknowledgement and in the full presence of a new Avatar of Shamballa.

Now, we will again come down into the great temple where you previously were. It is not often or usual that any earthman or even some of the higher realms of the astral world are permitted to send an emissary to view such a ceremony. However, due to the great importance of the age and of the time in which your planet is particularly situated at this moment, we thought perhaps that it might be of great value and of great importance to the peoples of your earth plane if they could see the progression of some such person who had lived on their planet at one time; and though he came to the earth people in the position as a humble servant and as a teacher, in the end he made a wonderful and a complete demonstration of the immortal nature of man, the inner self, and was a triumph over time and over evolution.

Now as we have emerged into the central temple, you will see that it is strangely empty. Before when we came in, it was filled to completion; however, let us sit quietly here for a few moments and I believe the ceremony is about to begin. I may say to you that these ceremonies may seem to be lacking in some of the fanfare or trumpeteering and the other various noises which are associated with your earth ceremonies. We leave nothing here to the more demonstrative parts of nature as they have been completely eliminated through the evolution of time. I do not mean to convey the impression that we are entirely expressionless—far from it. We live and enjoy life in a much fuller and a more complete fashion than it is possible for your earth minds to conceive. Now as we have been talking, you will see that the entrances which lead from the seven great spokes which surround this great temple have been filled with some sort of a strange light, inasmuch as this light seems to be coming out of these great passageways or corridors.

Now we will begin to see that there are a great number of forms or shapes which are standing just within the portals of these great corridors. Soon all will be in readiness. Now we are again hearing the chanting sing-song of the energies. Slowly in unison and marching abreast, the people emerge from the various radiating spokes or corridors. Each of these corridors, of course, represent the particular Shamballa from whence these souls came for this particular observance. As they march slowly down the steps, through the aisles, past the seats toward the great center cubicle which stands alone in the center of the temple, they are seemingly chanting the song of this vibrant energy. Louder and louder grows this song until it seems to be almost deafening in its intensity. When the ranks of the foremost leaders of the files of these people reach the bottom of the steps just in front of the altar, they all pause momentarily, then gradually they begin to file singly into the rows between the seats. Thus it is that they fill the seats up completely. However, they have not been seated yet. They are all standing. As you saw the demonstration of the projection of the radiant energy before and of its blinding intensity, now this seems to supersede and eclipse this previous demonstration. Slowly, from the great corner projectors, there seems to rise a wall of radiant lambent flame, which is of an immense white radiation. This seems to meet in the center and in converging has added to it the various ingredients of mind forces which are projected to it from the countless thousands of souls who are standing in unison around the room.

Slowly this great mass of flame begins to take shape. Within, it seems to sparkle a cascading fountain of millions of tiny star-like flashes of light which are continually appearing and reappearing. This great flame is, in itself, one of tremendous intensity and seems to glow with all of the colors of the rainbow but yet remains at a particularly white glowing radiance. Slowly this flame begins to take shape. It is not the form of one human being but it is the form of two. Slowly the head, the arms, the lower limbs, the bodies begin to form. It is two figures standing close side by side. Slowly all of the energies seem to melt and become absorbed into these two bodies which are standing motionless within the center of the flame. As the intensities of the radiance is absorbed into the bodies, more and more of the general aspects of the form are visible.

Now I see that you are beginning to understand who these two people are. You saw them in the emergence from the temple in the center of the city of Azure. They are Sha-Tok and Erza. They have emerged here in the great center temple at Parhelion to take their new office. Now as they stand straight and motionless and the song of the flame has died down, the great masses of souls who are in the surrounding seats around this great center cubicle extend their right hand upward in a gesture. They hold their

251

hands aloft for some moments, then slowly the hand is withdrawn to their forehead, where they touch their forehead. They touch their lips and then they touch their heart. This is a pledge of consecration and of service to the Father and with the complete cooperation of the Lord Avatar, who was once your Jesus on the earth plane. He and His biune now rule supreme over the seven Shamballas.

So friends, my dear brothers and sisters, though you may be scattered far and wide over the earth plane as you read these words, let it be a personal message to each and every one of you, of the continuity of life, of the immortality of man's soul. Do not hesitate in your forward evolution, and though you may be involved in many flights and in many lives, do not lose sight of the sacred and consecrated mission which will always lead you closer to the great Central Vortex. Remember always the words of wisdom which He once spread in the gospel which was brought to the earth two thousand years ago. Remember the words of brotherly love which have been brought not only from his lips but from countless others who have come and gone upon the earth plane. Remember also that all of the elements and ingredients which are necessary for your own personal evolution are contained within your own consciousness. The search for man's higher self begins on the more and the lowest of the elemental planes and continues onward and upward; and even though we here in the centers of Shamballa know that as we can look down and see the places in our progression where we have been, so we can look upward and see the places where we have yet to go. This is the message of life. This is the message of the Creative God-Force which is within you. Until such further time, may God's love rest in your heart.

CHAPTER 35

A ray of love and greetings to you again, brothers and sisters of the earth plane. During the past events and in our transmissions, there may have been some things happening which have given rise to some perplexing problems in your mind. It is therefore that I return and that we will resume our transmission that we may best explain what has been happening as well as some of the more relative values pertaining to these things. As you have no doubt surmised by now, there have been some graduations or some changes in the various offices or in the leadership of the various sections of Shamballa. Some time ago, you witnessed the ascension of him who we call Sha-Tok and his affinity, Erza. You also witnessed their emergence again into the Central Shamballa in the ceremony a few hours ago.

Now, of course, there are other changes in the leadership of the various other centers which will, of course, follow in a natural sequence and order. However, we will discuss some of those later. At present, Master John is the Lord of Venus and the Lord over all Shamballa is he and she who we call Sha-Tok and Erza. The affinity of John is still on the earth. Now the problem of affinity or, as you call it, sex relationship may have been one of some question and so I will attempt to further explain such relationship. In the book of Venus this was touched upon somewhat, however, I do believe that we may carry this explanation into a somewhat different perspective and thus gain a more relative or objective view.

It might be said that man, in the beginning of his evolution, does evolve in a separated state of consciousness or that he may be what you may call opposing polarities or exactly opposite counterparts of himself. This you have called male and female. Actually, in a pure spiritual sense, such elements that enter into the various characteristic potentials of each individual are thus manifest in an exact proportion in an opposite direction in another individual, who is, in either case, the male or female. Thus it is that through the countless evolutions of man's life upon the earth, he is continually revolving into such a relationship with his exact opposite polarity that he can obtain an objective relationship with this opposite polarity.

I do not like the word sex, as it has certain materialistic impingements which relate to the possessive qualities or the dominating qualities of man's nature in a physical dimension and is also only related to that procreative factor which is necessary in some earth plane existence. I will use instead the word centric. Thus on your earth plane you know many people who express different concepts of sex. You may have monocentrics, biocentrics, triocentrics and quadrocentrics. In a more normal relationship, life in the social structures of your earth plane is expressed as biocentric, or through the commonly accepted laws of marriage where one man marries a woman. In your Oriental countries, however, you very often see the concept of quadrocentric or even a multiple number of such attractions expressed in the various harems which have existed in these Oriental countries. In your own country, you no doubt know of the many monocentrics which, of course, revolve around among themselves and are only the consequence of one generation, as they seldom reproduce themselves. You may also know of other examples of quadrocentricity in which certain couples may display some affinity toward each other and live in very close relationship. They may even exchange their wives or their husbands. Other such examples of evolution in the consciousness of the relationship of man toward woman or woman toward man or the opposing polarities of man's nature may be expressed as mother and son or as daughter and father. The combinations here are, of course, innumerable but all in themselves express this same relationship toward one another in their evolution. In other words, by going through these countless evolutions and in these various aspects and in all these relationships, the sum and total which resolve into themselves as a direct and more harmonious relationship in a spiritual sense will supersede any of the physical experiences with himself.

In the final conclusion of evolutions into the spiritual worlds, man will thus find himself properly attracted to his own affinity and in this he is neither male nor female but expresses a perfect balance and quality of virtues or characteristics in each counterpart. So it was with Sha-Tok and Erza, and while you may have seen them in somewhat of the personality form of male or female as it was most commonly envisioned on your earth plane, yet this is not necessarily so. They are expressing in a pure spiritual sense this perfect combination and relationship of values toward one another. This is done purely in the spiritual sense, and inasmuch as there are no physical attributes or remembrances attached to these particular states of evolution, so it will be that while these two personalities may appear or reappear in the different centers of Shamballa at such times as is necessary for their appearance, they may come singly or they may come together. Yet, all in all, they will express this same perfect relationship and balance and harmony in all things which they do. Wherever it is that we find our need or our want and that we express the thought toward them, so they shall appear to help solve our problems.

I might add that in the days following their ascension from the plane of Venus, they were taken to a much higher dimension wherein certain orders were entered into and they were initiated into a much higher and a much enlarged state of consciousness. Thus they were able to return to the centers of Shamballa in a slightly altered, or as I shall say, a slightly higher state of consciousness and they also manifest this in such appearances as they may have among us. We do not, in a general sense of the word, attach the name personality to either or any of us; however, we are, for purposes of identification to the earth minds which render it necessary for such identification. We have superseded such usages by a more advanced state of relationship which unites us to them in a frequency relationship. By turning the dial of your radio, your radio does not need to know the name of the radio station. It only knows the law of frequency relationship. So it is with us in relating ourselves to our fellow beings here in these centers. We do not call them by a name but merely relate ourselves to them through this same law of harmonic relationship.

In the future, in your prayers and in the prayers of your fellow countrymen, while you may pray to your Father in heaven in such manner as best motivated by your own concept and you may inscribe the name of Jesus, the Christ, as the divine motivating power behind such prayer, yet truly these prayers shall find their proper place, and there is a proper receptacle for such prayers to be received in accordance with the strength and in accordance with the wish and desire of those who are praying. Let me say that your thoughts or your prayers are very necessary and very relative in our expression toward your earth plane and in other earth planes. This is a source of energy supply which is more nearly related to your own dimension and is much more readily usable in such form. It is also the constructive energies of your mind which relates you, in the direct law of harmonic frequency relationship, to those for and with whom you pray. So therefore, in the sum and total of such expressions, we can thus more directly utilize and properly focus such powers as are contained in these mind energies which you call prayers.

Therefore, let your prayers or your meditations be of such nature that they are strong perceptions and that in them you are conceiving such perfect conditions for your fellow man. Let not your prayers be of such selfish nature or motivated by your own self-interest, for such prayers are useless. Thus it is in our discussion here that we have been able to point out to you some of the various relative factors which are in actual sequence and often occur in the various evolutions of your earth life. I would not delude you by saying that marriages are not made in heaven. Marriages are purely the byproduct of such countless and innumerable evolutions in which each man and each woman find in themselves, and in these relationships in these various dimensions, the proper perspective of values, and in this evaluation they do arrive at the conclusion of their perfect marriage which is in heaven.

To my earth sister, she has properly guessed that this is not Leonardo. This is another person with whom you are not yet acquainted. In other words, I am the biune or biocentric part of Leonardo. I am she who you might call his soul mate. I will not impinge the consequence of my name into your consciousness because such name would mean little or nothing to you. I have evolved with him through the countless eons of time until we have arrived together in this plane of consciousness. Until such further time that we will deem necessary to resume our transmissions, may I say to you that we are all expressing our greatest and strongest concentrations and rays of energies of love in your direction.

CHAPTER 36

Greetings again from Parhelion. This is Leonardo speaking again and I am glad that you enjoyed our previous transmission this morning on a more proper evaluation of what is called sex. However, since that time there has been some discussion as to the presentation of some of the various factors which were explained to you in the opening chapters of our transmission. These related to our particular orbit and to such phraseology as might give the implication that we were actually traveling through space. This is not so.

As we have gone a considerable distance into the abstract sense, we feel that we must further explain certain things so that they will be more conducive to a general line of thinking. We will first attempt to confine our evaluation, even though it is highly abstract, into such terminology as can be understood by the largest number of the earth people. We here on Eros do not as in the case of the planet Venus confine ourselves into an orbit around a sun, nor do we have an orbit which would enable us to travel through space, just as your earth or Venus travels around the sun. If we can picture for a moment a little more abstract equation and that our orbit, as we have called it, is actually an oscillation. To best understand this particular situation, we will again refer to the chords on the piano and that while we are playing a high chord, we can also, with our left hand, play various low chords which are either in harmony or out of harmony with our original high chord. This was given to you in a previous transmission. Now, in explaining what we call an orbit, this merely means that we are actually standing still in what the scientist calls free space. As we have explained free space as a dimension which is unrelative to your own earth plane and that free space does not actually exist in the equated term of the earth scientist, we are therefore standing in free space; and because our planet is constantly changing at regular intervals its frequency rate or vibration, this automatically places it in different positions throughout the celestial universe. This can be termed, in a sense, an orbit. It merely means that in the pulsation or the frequency of our planet, we come into relative vibrationary contacts with the various planets with which we are associated. We can, at will, also change the rate of vibration or frequency of this planet so that we can recur, as it were into such positions in this oscillating orbit that will be most conducive to conducting some of the things which are relevant to our particular office.

Thus it was at the time of the birth of Jesus who is now our Lord Avatar upon your earth planet two thousand years ago. Actually there was no movement of our planet. We merely changed the frequency rate of the planet so that it came into a relative or a harmonious position with your planet which was partially or wholly seen as a guiding star by some of the earth people in that particular vicinity at that particular time. Now I believe that clears up this situation somewhat, so we must therefore understand that Eros as a whole is somewhat of a more spiritually evolved planet than any of the other six cities of Shamballa.

This will also explain to you something in the

nature of how it is possible that the various peoples of the other Shamballas are able to emerge or to travel back and forth from their particular relative planet. This also is simply a question of frequency alteration in which they too assume, temporarily at least, the vibration of our own planet and thus they are immediately within our particular position. This is of course a very highly evolved state of what is called radio or television transmission on your earth plane, inasmuch as the participants themselves are the active, integrated wave transmissions.

In other words, in your television program if it were possible for you to so change the frequency relationship of the actors and actresses who were enacting some scene in a television broadcasting studio, they would be projected on the beam and come directly into your living room and reenact their scene just as it was done in the studio. That is something of an allegory in which we are trying to explain the position of the planet Eros in regard to the other six centers of Shamballa. It will also in a large sense of the word explain to the earth scientist what he has long been trying to evaluate in his concept of time and space. Such things in a dimension of which we are a part do not exist in the relative sense in which he is familiar. These conditions like everything else about the earth plane are entirely of a different nature. Therefore, in the future, may I say to the earth scientist that he must change his evaluation of the various constituents of his wisdom or knowledge pertaining to such physical sciences which are relative to his earth plane. He will never arrive at a definite conclusion or an equation of space travel or of any other particular factors which have, up until the present time, chained him to the surface of his earth, and he will never break those chains until he changes the evaluations and equations of energy and mass.

Do not feel neglected, my brother, because you were not welcomed either in Venus or in Eros with, shall I say, a brass band and with fanfares and trumpets; you were welcomed nevertheless fully and with open arms by every one of us in every one of these cities at the time of your arrival. You were thus welcomed each time that you appear with all the love which we can manifest. However, you must remember that the frequencies in your psychic body have not yet resolved themselves into such a plane of consciousness that they would be entirely in harmony with the vibrations of our own planetary system which is Shamballa.

We have therefore refrained from entering into such active conversations or meetings with the various personalities in these planets for the very obvious reason that it might be not only confusing but damaging. So therefore, in the future, our particular transmissions and explorations of the various centers shall continue in a more or less unobtrusive fashion that will meet with the least resistance on your own part and will meet with the least resistance by the minds and mentalities of the earth people. Our purpose here primarily is to explain what is the function and nature of these centers and not to necessarily meet the various personalities or people who are so engaged in either the controlling destinies of these centers or in the pursuance of their various duties or activities. You will appreciate our position also that we do not like the personality ego attached to any of our particular endeavors, so therefore we do not actively engage in such endeavors which might bring us into the limelight of public observance. We will in the fullest measure of our understanding and in the humblest capacity toward the source and supply of all things, render such services and such things as we possibly can which will better and further the purpose of whatever particular earth you may find yourself.

I would also like to clear up a little bit further on some of the dimensions of this particular city of Parhelion. As it was mentioned rather vaguely before that, it covered several hundred square miles. This is quite true. The city of Parhelion would very easily cover any of your largest earth cities and leave a lot over to spare. However, such dimensions as to cities might also confuse the earth minds if they were brought down into the terminology in which they could understand, as miles, feet or inches. We will only say that this great city is sufficient unto the size and needs for which it was so designed. The buildings which comprise the spokes and the rim and the central temple themselves are quite high and probably at least as high as your tallest skyscraper. These are divided into various levels or floors as you might call them. So you can begin to see that this is a city of tremendous and vast size and indeed it must needs be so, for it is servicing not only your earth planet but is servicing many other thousands of planets in such similar positions throughout our galaxy or star cluster. This it does as it will be further explained and enlarged upon in the various capacities which comprise this central educational system of the Shamballa.

Other questions might arise; you may think that we are necessarily slaves to our position. Indeed not. When you change the perspective and the evaluation of your life into such semblance and conformity as will make it universal in the service of the brotherhood, you will find that your greatest joy and pleasure is in the service of others. You will not need to relax the physical mind from such torturous systems as are involved in your present-day material civilization. Such relaxations must necessarily occur for the physical minds would otherwise be seriously warped and distorted. Such pressures do not exist in our world as the abundant and supreme supply of God's wisdom, which is our Fountainhead or Central Vortex, supplants every need which might be similarized to the earth-man's equation. In other words, we simply do not suffer the fatigue which you might necessarily associate with the continual, as you would call it, working with our various factors and segments in our relative functions to these planetary systems.

I hope that I have somewhat cleared up these various questions in your mind and until such further pursuance, may I remain with all the love from every one of us here in Parhelion.

CHAPTER 37

Now we are progressing step by step toward a more absolute and, shall I say, abstract concept of what is called time-space or energy transference in various dimensional factors. In the beginning it was said our planet traveled in orbit. Later it was explained that such an orbit was not a physical sense of traveling as you do in the earth plane or as an evolution around some particular distance of space but rather, a pulsation or a frequency which occurred as a major cycle of about thirty-eight hundred years duration. It was also explained that such frequency alteration could change the relative perspective point of the planet in regards to the various expressions which were necessary in manifesting such portions or parts as were deemed necessary to the various planetary systems.

Now to further evaluate this more absolute concept, let us create some allegorical equations with which you are more familiar. If we take a large pail and a hose which is attached to a faucet and after placing the end of the hose against the side of the pail, we will cause the water to run into the pail. If this is done slowly enough, the water will start revolving around in the pail in a circular fashion. If we toss in a few small chips or bits of sawdust, we will see that these small chips gradually revolve round and around until they converge into the center of the circular form or mass of water. Thus you have seen expressed two very fundamental physical laws. They are called centrifugal force and centripetal force. Centrifugal force means in the physical relationship that such masses are cast away by a revolving force, such as mud flying from the wheel of your auto. Centripetal force means that such liquid substance on a revolving disc will be attracted toward the center because of the fact that less energy is consumed with a decreasing diameter of the time it takes the liquid mass to move. If we speed up the circular motion of the water in our pail by increasing the flow of water from the hose, it will revolve fast enough so that the flat plane of water seems to be dipped in a cone-like manner toward the center. The little particles of wood will thus, through the force of gravity, increase their speed toward the center. This is the third factor which is quite important to remember in our further equations.

Now we will bring our attention and focus it upon another more relative earth plane expression which can be similarized to a storage battery in your automobile. There you have two poles. One is positive and one is negative. Here centrifugal force is expressed from the positive pole, that is, energy in a more electrical form flowing away from the positive pole. Centripetal force is expressed in the relationship of energy flowing into it. Gravity is thus expressed as the law of attraction which balances these two forces. Now if we can extend our equation up into a still higher realm or dimension, we can start first with your more familiar earth atom. Here we might say is a small space which is revolving in a pulsating manner. It is not space in a pure sense but is actually energy. As it pulsates it draws in energy from a higher dimension and in such pulsation in a circular form just as the pail of water; the energies of which it is composed will regenerate such smaller and smaller or negative fractions in the law of harmonic relationship. These smaller and smaller energies will decrease and decrease toward the center until there is formed a nucleus or a hard core mass of negative energies.

Now this energy must always travel and must go somewhere. If we can pause a moment right here and draw a similar equation in your earth plane again, I will point out if you will take a piece of paper and a

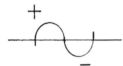

pencil and draw an elongated S. At the top of the S, you will place a plus mark or a positive sign and at the bottom a minus. Then you will draw a line straight through the middle portion of the S. This is what you call a sine wave.

All energy in your third dimension of electrical nature or even a sound nature travels in such a form or fashion. We can see that energy traveling from the plus sign must pass through the negative portion in order to again become positive and positive back into negative. This is what we mean by alternating or reciprocating energy and this carried into a higher relationship or a higher dimension means actually the expansion and contraction of the great voids of space which aren't space at all but are actually filled with radiant energies so expressing themselves in a continual pulsating positive and negative fashion.

Now to continue our earth plane equation, we will begin with the atom. As it was explained, energy will come from a higher dimension in a pulsating nature and in such a cycular form as was demonstrated in the pail of water. It will form and reform the smaller and smaller or more negative forms of energy to a hard core nucleus. We might say that this looks something like a rather flattened cone. At the apex of this cone is a very hard concentrated mass of negative energies. This is what you call the nucleus of the atom. Now this energy must go somewhere so that it must reform itself in a positive fashion. This it does in expressing itself into your third dimension as its own particular relative element. Thus it maintains its characteristics irrespective of anything that you may try to do to change it, simply because you cannot change it from your side of the plane. In other words, the atom now is expressing a certain relative quotient of intelligence; thus it is an element and remains so irrespective of what other things may be done to it. Your solar system is merely a blown-up equation of the atom. The sun is actually the center core or nucleus of the tiny, more negative wave forms which have resolved themselves through the lines of force which extend out beyond the limits of your last planetary orbit.

It is this pulsating energy which comes into the plane of your dimension which you call your solar system. In revolving around and around in the pulsating fashion of frequencies, it regenerates and regenerates in the law of harmonic relationship such frequencies or exact multiples of itself, something like the chords on the organ. These energies continually revolve through centripetal force, as you might call it, in the lower earth-plane equation, toward the center. This centripetal force thus has gathered unto itself the hard core energies which you call your sun.

Now, centrifugal force must again express itself in a higher law or a higher dimension. Thus in a lower dimension the negative now becomes positive. The centrifugal force becomes the positive equation of the storage battery, so energy flows out into your third dimensional world. This is again contacted by the planets in a similar fashion to that of the atom. Actually your planets are hardcore nucleuses of the same form and structure as the atom. From each planet is a great mass or field of energy which is in a lower dimension from the preceding one above it. In revolving and revolving around and around, it in turn regenerates the smaller and smaller negative wave forms which condense through centripetal force as (we will call this equation) into what you call your planet. Thus again, energy is expressing itself in an infinite number of ways into your planet which, in thus expressing themselves into your planet, again become positive equations of such relative mass and energy as compared to the plane from whence it had just arisen. Thus you will begin to see the linkage all the way through the countless dimensions on down. You will also begin to understand that when such intelligence is interrupted in any particular way or form, it might even manifest itself as cancer in your body.

Now as far as our own personal planet is concerned, Eros might be said to be the cone or hard-core nucleus of a great central vortex which has been called the vortex, or the Fountainhead, by the Venusians. We, in this great central city of Parhelion, are merely expressing the same law of, from negative to positive equations, as we have just discussed. In other words, the energies, which are pouring down into this planet from a great central vortex or mass of energy from a tremendously high and elevated dimension, do so and expand into this planetary form or hard nucleus. Thus it is, we have constructed our city at the exact point of contact and emergence from this great central revolving vortex. We therefore express energy in seven different relative planes which resume themselves in a form just as your planetary system does in various spiritual planets which are scattered around throughout your celestial galaxy of stars. This is a wide circular band of seven planets. Now if you can count up past seven, you will begin to think that there are eight instead of seven centers including Eros.

Again we may make an earth plane equation. We shall say there is a mother hen who is white and has seven chicks, one of which is white. The other six are of different colors. We therefore express ourselves in a more personal relationship into a lower plane which is similar or compatible to the other six centers of Shamballa. The other six centers, in turn, express themselves in the same relative equation or expression of such science. Now we will not confuse ourselves with the word science. Science in your earth plane understanding merely means something with which you have associated test tubes or microscopes or with something of that nature. However, this is not exactly so. There is nothing which you do on your earth plane or that you will ever do on any other earth plane that is not scientific if it is expressed correctly.

There is science in everything. There is science in the way the painter mixes his paints and spreads them upon the canvas. There is science in the way that the poet composes the various lines or stanzas of his verse and in the meter in which he expresses his thoughts. There is a great deal of science in music and in the reproduction of music and composition. Thus it is, we cannot ever separate ourselves from science because science is the actual integrated and the most intelligent working concept of any particular thing which we enter into. It thus becomes scientific. So therefore, you will begin to understand how closely interwoven these various factions are which are expressed from Shamballa to the various earth planes and the various countless thousands of solar systems throughout the galaxy of the universe. I might also in speaking of this universe say that as your earth astrophysicist has pictured it as something like a vast radiating pinwheel, this will illustrate some form of what we have already discussed, inasmuch as this is the lower or the more relative physical plane of expression.

Just above this great vortex of starry clusters which seem to radiate or stem in a pinwheel fashion from a central vortex is another dimension. The central vortex of the universe you have thus pictured is actually the point or the cone on which rests this great spiritual dimension which is revolving about it in a cycular fashion. It is the regeneration and regeneration again of the negative wave forms of energy which precipitate into the central vortex and stem out into the radial lines of your universe and thus re-manifest themselves in countless galaxies of suns and planetary systems. The energy or the intelligence is likewise carried through in many other dimensions of expression and thus becomes the various and innumerable types of life upon each one of these planets or in the number of the stars or the suns, as they are more properly called, in the expression of these similar vortexes as that we have just discussed.

In pointing out these facts to the earth scientist, if you will carefully evaluate these things and with such proper necessary diagrams or mathematical equations which I am not attempting to interject at this moment, you will begin to form a basis for the new science for your New Age. Your New Age will not and cannot be made possible until such proper evaluations are made. In your world you have a law you call the law of diminishing returns. You have long since reached that point and passed it in your science. Because of the fact that you have left out certain relative spiritual values which link you on and on up through the infinities of the various vast, shall I say, dimensions which surround you, you have therefore built up this preponderance or the false structure of the material appurtenances about you. So in the evolution of the next few hundred years of mankind upon your earth plane, you will begin to understand what a star is, what a planetary system is, what an atom is, what causes so many other innumerable mysteries which you have tried to solve, and falsely tried to solve them from your earth plane position which is utterly impossible.

In our previous discussion I made some statements which are apt to be challenged and arouse a good deal of controversy. I stated that in the natural order of atoms that it was quite impossible to change atomic structures. In an absolute concept, this is quite true. I am, of course, speaking of what has been called transmutation or changing from one element to another through some laboratory process. Now you say you have atomic bombs, such as fissionable or thermonuclear types. In either case, however, you have merely succeeded in so stretching or changing such atomic structures into an unnatural and unrelated perspective with their true source or dimension. Thus it is in triggering these atoms by some other smaller explosion, they, in trying to adjust themselves to their natural source or perspective, actually blow themselves to pieces. This is not atomic power. You may point out you have atomic reactors. This, too, means that you are more slowly destroying atoms.

A much more constructive evaluation of atomic power would be one in which the elements were not destroyed, rather, they became the channel through which the higher dimensional force was properly utilized. Each atom would thus in turn become a tiny power plant which would not be destroyed or degenerate but instead, transfer into your dimension a direct relative equation of energy into some usable form. This you have approached much closer in realization in what you call the great cyclotrons or other types of such electronic and magnetic properties which precipitate a tremendously accelerated stream of energy into such substance as cobalt. The atoms of cobalt therefore take on new superimposed wave forms within their vortexes which are gradually discharged over the period of time. They are thus said to be made radioactive. This, as I have said, is a much closer and a truer relationship of atomic power than you have achieved in your so-called atom bombs or your atomic reactors.

We do not become intelligent in our purposes to change things to suit our purpose or that we would not go around smashing things, nor would we take the iron ore from the earth and attempt in such a similar fashion to construct such as your necessities of life, the skyscraper, or the automobile. Iron in this case has been changed somewhat in its original molecular state by the addition of thermal energy and of other various types of minerals into the constituents of steel. However, the true atom of the iron has in no way been changed. Thus, all through the scale of your atomic elements, you do not change by adding to or taking away any of the particular atomic constituents of that element. I will not say that this has not been done on your earth plane but wherever it has been done, whether on your earth plane or in other earth planes, it must be done from an entirely different angle than by simply attempting to blow such atomic structures apart. It must be done from, shall I say, the more highly evolved or elevated spiritual concepts of life. I might add and point out that should you ever arrive at the conclusion of your atomic experiments and include an absolute and complete misuse of atomic power, you will no doubt reduce your little earth planet into a cosmic cloud of dust. Therefore, I would like to caution and warn you to the utmost that you must approach these things in a much more sensible evaluation.

In our previous discussions you will begin to see the sequence of such planes or dimensions as we have called them, and in their relative appearance and reappearance as negative and positive planes of expression, that you, in your atomic experiments of destruction and blowing apart, are sometimes quite seriously interrupting such natural sequences. These are, of course, very relative to your earth plane existence. You may find in a hundred years or so that you are producing nothing more or less than a race of malformed mutants. You may also wonder why your vegetation will no longer support your way of life. In this you have already partially passed the borderline. I might point out that these things all lie without the immediate vision of your perspective. You have not yet evaluated such proper frequency spectrums that lie beyond your immediate relative plane of existence. Just as in sunlight, you have not yet properly evaluated that sunlight does not exist beyond your earth plane in the perspective of sunlight or heat, as you evaluate it on the surface of your planet. And so in consequence, these things are constantly increased in magnitude as they obtain a higher and higher perspective in relationship to your earth plane.

To your earth scientists, I would urge you to appeal to your governmental influences into the utmost capacity to discontinue in their urge or their need to construct more fearful weapons against some fancied adversary. Likewise, to those who are across the sea,

I would urge you also to discontinue this mad race to oblivion for surely that is where it will lead you if you continue on in your atomic experiments just as you have been doing in the past few years. There will be some time or other some one or a group of scientists who will come along, who will be sped by the impetus of these false experiments to the point where they have actually triggered your whole earth to pieces. So therefore friends and brothers and sisters on the earth plane, please be united and concerted in your efforts to stop this mad and continued race to oblivion.

Faraday

* A later transcription related this English inventor and scientist—who was the discoverer of electromagnetic induction, or magnetism, on the earth about 1831, then named Faraday—to have been the reincarnate of Pericles, who lived in the Grecian era about 600 B.C.

CHAPTER 38

Greetings, welcome again to Eros. From across the vast distances of space we come to you and while it is not space but filled with radiant energies, let us watch while we see something like a searchlight beam which seems to be forming and stealing softly across this void. It comes into your minds and it enfolds you swiftly, softly and silently and you are taken back here to us so that we again stand before one of the great entrances to the magnificent city of Parhelion. As you watch about you carefully, you will see much that is wonderful, beautiful and fills you with a great awe, for the planet itself is something like a huge luminous globe which seems to lift and fall with its radiant energies changing as it does from one of the many hued colors of the rainbow into another, and that all of the things about you are likewise glowing and pulsating in unison with this wonderful radiating power which comes from seemingly nowhere.

I will talk a moment while your eyes become accustomed to looking about you. I will ask that you will be a bit patient with my tongue for I have not used it in your earth-plane language for many thousands of years. Now you are standing before a gate or an entrance over which there is the symbol of an ancient musical instrument which is called the lyre and, as you have correctly surmised, you are about to enter into the portal which is devoted to the cultural arts of not only your earth plane but of the countless other earth planes in similar positions throughout the galaxies of the universe. The arts I am referring to are music, drama, literature, sculpturing and painting. I believe I named them correctly. As is the case with the other entrances of this great city, you must pass through the portals which will condition you in a way whereby you may be able to see something of the nature of the culture and of the sciences, if I can call them such loosely.

This section of the city is devoted to such cultivation and to such enlarging of these respective arts or cultures in the earth planes. I have not made my name known yet and so, I will beg the kindness of your indulgences with me. May I say I am just he who you called Kung Fu (Confucius) on your earth planet and that I had collected together some of the truths which were expressed in my native Chinese some many years ago on your earth planet. So as I have said, I am not too familiar with your 'Engliss'. It may be possible a little later on that someone may resume the privilege of conducting you through the planet which is devoted to the cultures of your earth plane. We believed it best that we bring you here directly to Eros and Parhelion so that you may start from here as the distances or as the change in vibration which is more correct to interpret, is of a considerable change as this particular planet is in a rather peculiar position in our galaxy of stars. I may say that as we pass into the entrance which is dedicated to the arts and sciences of the world that you will see several of my fellow countrymen. One you knew as Lao-tse, also, Master Hilarion is here and rules this section of Shamballa.

Now let us pass through the portal and go into the foremost of the laboratories which is devoted to teaching and to the cultivation in the higher spiritual senses of these arts and cultures. There is a difference here in the former section of science which you previously visited inasmuch as you will now see that not only do you feel differently but all things about you are also of a much different character. Before, in the former section, things were devoted to science in a more pure and relative sense and were constantly bathed in a white light which also gained its strength from some of the longer rays which your earth scientist call the infrared spectrum.

Here, in this particular section, however, we are using some of the more subtle of the stimulating shades of colors which go into the pinks and coral shades. Color, however, is of a different nature and of a different expression than what you normally associate color with on your earth plane. There it is something you use merely as a convenience for identification of objects around you so that you may, as you term it, see. Here we do not have physical eyes inasmuch as physical eyes would be useless as all frequency spectrums are of a much higher order and relationship. Your physical eye would not respond to any of the colors we have here. Color here means that it is the basic, shall I say, the emanating source or the strongest radiating force which determines the nature of the particular function which we do in these various centers. We may also say that the same particular color is dominant in the planetary systems in which we teach and express.

Now that we are more firmly inside the building and walking into some of the great rooms which are in the front part or section which is the periphery of the rim, we will come into a great cathedral-like room which is several hundred feet high and many hundreds of feet wide. At the far end of this great cathedral-like room is a huge and massive pipe organ, something similar to those you may see in a great cathedral on your earth plane. Here it is that we teach something of the relative functions of such type of vibrotherapy which is necessary to the healing processes which are stimulated through the various organs and centers of the human earth bodies who go into the churches where these organs are. As the student progresses through his studies, he is made aware of the nature and the intensity of sound and of its action in the various nerve centers of the body. He is also made aware of such resonant chords and sound structures as will best serve his purpose.

I might tell you that the Master who is presiding over this particular section or room is a great composer on your earth plane who flourished and was known as Johann Sebastian Bach. It is he who teaches here with his students who will make their appearance in some of the earth planes in the future. I see you are gazing rather in wonder and awe at this organ. Yes, indeed it supersedes anything that you have seen, even in your great Salt Lake tabernacle as the pipes themselves are made of some pure crystal-like substance which you have become familiar with in these various planets and that these various long pipes are assuming more strange and fantastic patterns and lengths and dimensions than you had ever believed possible. I might point out too that the crystal structures themselves give peculiar qualities which are unheard and unnoticed by your earth ears nor could they be properly identified by such ears as they exist in your human bodies. Yes, even the floor and the seats about you seem to be of some very beautiful pastel shade of pink which seems to be very stimulating and yet very pleasing and has the feel to your sense of being very soft to touch mentally, if I can say it as such.

Now come with me and we will go into one of the other rooms. Let us step through this nearby doorway here and we will enter into another one of the very large classrooms which is devoted to the art of drama. Here you will notice that the room is actually divided up into many sections and while there seems to be no visible partitions, yet there are definite partitions in a sense of the word. Here you will find that drama in its various expressions is being taught to the future teacher, who is at the present time a student. In the various relative earth plane expressions, he will in the future therefore find himself in such position that he will be able to give a much more and a correct interpretation of such particular plays or interpretations as are at the moment on your plane of expression.

Here we see the various interpretative forms of drama as they exist either in terpsichore or in the spoken word or in such phases as acting out the various interpretations, either silently or with the voice or with the song. Some of these have been, of course, written by great masters—Rossini, Verdi, Puccini and various other composers and musicians who lived on your earth hundreds of years ago. There are, of course, other teachers and masters who have come from other planets which are scattered around in the various planetary systems. As you can see, this room itself stretches away until it is almost invisible in the distance, it is so large. There is one thing that we would like to impress you with here, or those who read these lines, is of the vast size and the immense nature of all the things which are being done here. I am giving you something of a synopsis which will enable you to best enjoy and to view later on, the actual existence of the planet under whose control this section of Parhelion exerts its will. There are closely connected here also other large classrooms which relate to various other phases of teaching in the field of music, of the written word or literature, such as stories, plays, historical narrations, which are of the more intellectual expressions of the physical man.

Now here is another large classroom which is devoted to the teaching of such forms of prose and poetry. As you will see, this particular room is especially softly radiant, much more so than any of the others. You would naturally associate classrooms with desks or such paraphernalia as would be found in the schoolrooms of the earth, however, this is not so. Almost all classrooms, if we can call them such, are not actually classrooms in the sense of the word that you would associate with your earth plane classrooms. Instead, they are expressive of their own particular art or science which is being taught there. For instance, here in this large room which is devoted to poetry, to prose and to such of the finer of the more literate arts, we find scenes which are of extreme pastoral beauty. We find the most beautiful verdant gardens which is possible to imagine. We find bowers which are covered with rose blossoms; we find pools of clear liquid crystal-like water; we find huge moss-covered stones and the softest grass. We find everything which is conducive to stimulating the more esthetic nature of the student and the teacher. There are none of the drab bare classroom appearances which you might associate with this particular expression of art.

I would like to point out that your modern educational systems would benefit much by changing the drabness of your classrooms into something which was a little more conducive to the more pure intellectual inflow and outflow of thought transference. As in the case of the room with the large pipe organ, there, too, you saw everything which was of the inspirational nature which you would attach to such a magnificent display of music and its reproductive mechanism.

Let us pass across the hall and enter into another room or a large section which is devoted to the expression or art of sculpturing. In your various earth planes, you will see much of this science. It is very necessary that mankind in the material planes should know of the proper usage of stone, not only in his ability to carve such shapes as may be suggestive of the human form but he must also carve or emblazon such insignia or shape such into suitable building materials for temples or other edifices.

So it has always been thus through the pages of history that man is constantly associating himself with such a craft as carving the stone of the earth. In the ancient civilization of Egypt, they were very adept at this art and knew how to harden their copper tools so that they were almost as good as the steel ones which are in use today. The ancient Egyptian was very clever in this type of science and he has left great edifices of stone which have endured through the countless centuries and will endure for countless more. So the art of stone or sculpturing is not necessarily confined to the carving of some statue which may grace a museum but includes many of the various expressions which are attached to such processes which use the natural stone of the earth planets.

In this room, however, you will not see any of the students actually using such things as mallets or chisels or any of the other laborious manipulative processes which you would customarily associate with this expression. Instead, he is studying and placing within his own mind the various fundamental concepts which are necessary to his expression.

Later on, in his physical body on some earth plane, he will be intuitively aware of what to do in such a particular instance or he may develop some new process which will make him an outstanding exponent of his particular expression of sculpturing.

There are other sections of this particular portion of Parhelion which are devoted to such of the arts as the composition of music. Here again you will find that the students are not hammering out their learning on some piano keyboard, neither do they use any of the other stringed or repercussive instruments. Instead, they are studying the fundamental sciences which involve proper tone combinations, consonance of values which are relative and conducive to various types of harmony. He, like the sculptor, will also find in his future earth plane existences new and creative ways of expressing his compositions which will make him outstanding in his field. I might say that all of your great earth-plane musicians received such training here many hundreds or even thousands of years before they made their emergence in your earth plane. If I were to name even a half dozen or more, you would recognize them all instantly as those who have created the great masterpieces of the symphonies and of the operas which have endured through the ages.

I might also name many others who have contributed equally great contributions to the posterity of mankind in your earth planes who have also received their teaching here before emerging in your earth plane. Your encyclopedia would furnish you with hundreds, yes even thousands of these names. You could start with Shakespeare and go on down through the list with such men as Browning, Keats, Shelley, Longfellow, not to mention innumerable others. Great painters have also gone through this section—Landseer, Van Dyke, Michelangelo and a host of others which would read like a 'Who's Who' in your encyclopedia.

Again I must extend my humblest pardon for not being familiar with your 'Engliss' language. It is with great difficulty that we are even conveying one small fraction of what actually goes on here in this great city of Parhelion. However, as time goes by and such sections are added to your knowledge, you will begin to understand something of the vastness and scope of actually what goes on here and yet, my dear ones, may I say that even Eros and Parhelion is just one small part of such expressions through the vast cosmos you have called a universe.

It is as we have named it in your earth language, Parhelion, which means a bright spot on a halo, and as such it is, just a small bright spot on a halo. Our purpose is to impress you with the magnitude of the intelligent nature of the great Force you call God. This is extremely difficult but it must be so because of the Second Coming of what you call Christ and that the coming of Christ is not the coming of a personality but is the coming of a great new infusion of Spirit and intelligence into your world, where you will begin to live in such a way that you will begin to be spiritually interconnected with your fellowman. Each and every one of you will then express some small portion of the Christ. That will be the Second Coming. Now I see the power is dwindling so may we rest with God's love.

CHAPTER 39

A hearty welcome to you here in our 'little' community of Parhelion and I see that you are again standing at the entrance to that particular part of this great city which is devoted to the higher forms of art which are so relative to your earth plane. I am speaking, of course, in continuance of the previous transmission which was given to you by Kung Fu, one of my worthy compatriots here in this particular section. I will introduce myself first as I was quite well known on your earth planet several hundred years ago and I believe I left a few little bits of writings around which you occasionally remember. I have been known as William Shakespeare. Let us not dawdle on the outside but come right on in. I know that you never cease to be amazed at the display of electronic pyrotechnics which you see about you each time you arrive. May I say that I have been here for hundreds of years and I still am thrilled at the continual recurrence of these displays of energies. To your earth people, your nearest thing which I could describe would be something like the Aurora Borealis or the Northern Lights which plays about the North Pole.

In the previous transmission, Kung Fu led you about to the various sections and a rather sketchy tour was instituted. I believe here that it will be to our advantage if we go into several of these centers and to more thoroughly examine just what it is that we call classrooms or various other centers of learning. We have continually tried to impress you with the tremendous size of these various centers which are divided in this great city, and this section of Muse, as you would call it, is no exception. Let us go first into this room which I have a particular affinity for as it is more relevant to that type of literature and the expression of the art known as drama on the earth plane. We will pass through this large doorway and enter into what has been previously called a room. As you will see, the word 'room' was used merely for lack of something more adequate. Looking above you first, the ceiling, if we can call it such, is something more than a hundred feet above you and that it does not possess the appearance of a ceiling in the commonly accepted word, rather it is a pulsating, throbbing conglomeration of brilliantly hued flowing colors which seem to stream back and forth in the immediate space above you so that you are not actually seeing any particular solid substance but rather, the living, breathing, pulsating energies, with which you have become somewhat familiar. Lowering your gaze down into the level about you, you will see also that the whole appearance of things before you takes on a very sylvan appearance. In other words, it looks like a tremendous flower garden or a horticulturist's dream.

Let us walk slowly down one of these pathways because a little further along I have something very wonderful to show you. As we pass by these many different types of flora and fauna, the beautiful trees, shrubs, plants and flowers, all growing in luxuriant profusion which defies description, you will think this is indeed a strange classroom and so it is. Occasionally, as we walk along through this pathway, we see benches or settees which are set back away from the path, something like they would be in your earth parks. Here it is that the students or instructors may pause momentarily for a moment's inspiration in whatever particular thing they are desirous of interpreting. As we will walk along this pathway, I would like to explain to you that many of the personages whom you will see from time to time, or that may be noted in these works, and as they all are more or less, shall I call them, advanced souls, you may be interested to know that they appeared on your earth plane from time to time in the natural sequence or order, as you call reincarnation. You might say that Archimedes reappeared later on in your earth plane as Albert Einstein or that you might say that many of the other old Grecian or pre-Grecian philosophers, even those who were of Egypt and China, have since reappeared from time to time in your earth plane.

Nor are they limited here. They could likewise appear and have appeared in other planes which are somewhat relative to your own earth existence. Although I have not appeared on your earth plane since I passed from there in my last reincarnation, I intend to reappear there shortly, within the next hundred years or so, as it will then be for many of us to help and assist in working out something of what you call your Aquarian Age.

Now that we have approached closer to the center, you will see that this vast parkway about you is becoming more open and there is not the seeming abundance or profusion of the plant life. Instead, you will see open spaces which are carpeted with a deep moss-like substance which seems to gleam and sparkle with all of the colors of the rainbow. But at last we are here. We are standing now and I see that you are gasping with amazement, for before you is rather a large bowl-shaped depression which is possibly something like two or three miles in diameter. Around and about this bowl are scattered innumerable small trees and shrubbery, moss-covered stones, settees and various other things which may be associated with the idea or thought of repose or a reclining position. Down near the center of the great bowl is a small circular lake which is filled with the same liquid crystal energies which you first saw tumbling on the rocks on the mountain on your first visit. In the center of this small lake is a huge flat-top stone of some glittering and glowing crystal substance from the center of which springs a beautiful cascading fountain.

On your earth, you have something I believe now which you call the dancing waters. As you will notice, the fountain which plays from this huge stone is of that nature and it cascades up and down and seems to dance in a variety of incandescent colors. You will also see about you stretched on the sides of the bowl-like depression innumerable personages who are my fellow students and who are also those who from time to time take over in a small way, with the idea of instructing. I have brought you here purposely at this time as there is to be, shall I say, a lecture given by one of the higher personages who is to come here today and deliver something of a lecture or a talk on some of the higher sciences in the composition of word-form languages which are used in the various earth planes. I would not give you this man's name as the name would mean nothing to you, as he has not appeared on your earth plane for several thousand years. He comes from another plane which deals primarily, or is relative to another group of physical earth planes in another part of the universe.

However, let us sit down here on this mossy bank and recline and wait for the proper time while appreciating something of the beauties of the scene before you. Now you will see that the beautiful cascading radiant fountain in the middle of the lake is slowly diminishing and finally dies away completely. There is now a strange hushed silence where a few moments before was the sing-song of the energies as they played from the fountain. Now this, too, has ceased. Suddenly there appears on the surface of the stone where the energies had just been playing a particularly beautiful form of something which looks like a large elongated flame. You are wondering whether this is a person. Yes, indeed, it is a person but one who you cannot see in a true dimension or form or size. This man is appearing here as he comes from one of the higher dimensions in which the more relative earth-plane expressions of form or dimension do not exist. In other words, he has long since ceased to need the use of arms or legs. Neither does he use eyes or vocal cords or any other of the physical appurtenances which are familiar to your physical body. Instead, he is a pure expression of an individualized form of divine energy as it comes from the Fountainhead. As you can easily see, he is much further advanced than we are here. In fact, he may, in a sense of the word, be further along the pathway than some of our more advanced leaders who are leading this particular portion of Shamballa.

Now you will see that this wonderful, beautiful glowing flame is something about ten feet in height, if I can use your familiar earth plane equations of measurements. As I said before, he presents no physical appearance as you would define a physical appearance, but you are immediately impressed in your mind with some sort of a tremendous intelligence, a very strong feeling of force which you have heretofore been somewhat cognizant of but have not yet fully appreciated. Here in this case with this personage he is, as he is so tremendously advanced, able to dissipate a tremendous amount of the radiant energies which are permeating your mind. This is the lecture. To you it means nothing but to the mental eyes and ears of those about you it means a vast deal more. It is sort of a catalystic agent or an energy which permeates their minds and which helps to shape up the various wave forms and vortexes which will go into making up what you call their intelligence. Later on as they evolve around in these various centers and to the point where they can visualize some sort of the science or the philosophy or any of the arts which they are in affinity to, they will wish to reincarnate onto some physical plane and thus become a teacher or an exponent of that particular expression they have learned here. The personage who you see before you on the huge center portion of the stone in the lake is projecting these energies into the minds of the thousands of students and teachers who are sitting about the bowl-like depression which stretches away from this little lake.

As you watch the personage as he stands there, the flame is not stationary but seems to move and throb and pulsate or oscillate in a continual succession of peculiar wave forms. There seems to be also, around the apex or the top part of the particular wave something which changes color in a rapid succession of frequencies. These colors run the gamut of all the known shades of the rainbow and a few hundred are added to this. These are actually, in an advanced form, the word forms which are propagated or projected into the minds of the students who are listening to this lecture. This lecture will go on possibly for something like fifteen or twenty minutes in your earth-plane time dimension. However, this is a very irrelevant factor and means little or nothing as time assumes an entirely different characteristic here on

Parhelion. Actually what may appear to be fifteen or twenty minutes to you on your earth plane could be a year or ten years here, as the difference is not in the time but in the amount of such things as are being done. The measurement of time means little or nothing here in the city of Parhelion. In other words we do not measure things in time, so that time becomes something which is not a necessity whereby we measure our lives but becomes more the quotient whereby we learn of the various things and do the various duties for what we have devoted our lives and our intelligence. But I see that there has been somewhat of a breakdown in our transmission and until we establish a more complete contact, let us discontinue here for a moment and pass into one of the other of the large rooms as by now the Master, as we will call him, has finished his particular lecture which he came here to do and has disappeared. In his place, the waters are again playing in their iridescent fashion upon the large stone in the center of the lake.

Come now, let us walk back up this pathway which is a shortcut back into another one of the more scientific centers. You will no doubt wonder as to how many of the musicians, the artists, poets and so on who have appeared on your earth plane which numbers many hundreds have learned of their particular art or science as they have expressed it. Many of these have been outstanding and before their time. There are very definite reasons why these things exist. We are pointing out to you that they must learn of these arts and sciences before they reincarnate into an earth plane. These, in turn, from these centers are in consequence learned from the higher Masters or Lords who come to us from even the higher planes above our particular planes of existence as they are expressed in these centers. So in the natural sequence or evolution of knowledge or wisdom, this is again a working out or manifestation of the Supreme Intelligence or radiating power which permeates from the Central Vortex.

Now we have arrived in this large particular portion which I will call a laboratory. You are immediately impressed, as I see, with a vast array of very weird and strange-looking apparatus which stretches out before you. Here again is a very large center which is devoted exclusively to the science of, as I shall call it, vibration or vibronics. Here students from all spiritual concepts in the various sciences are intermingled regardless of their particular expression, who are learning the more fundamental scientific concepts which go into the makeup of their own expression. Such as it is, though it is poetry or drama, there is a natural conclusive sequence of word forms which, in their proper usage, will start a series of wave train formations which is called sound. The sound, in impressing its intelligence in the various nerve centers of the brain of the human who is on the earth plane will immediately correlate such vibration with previous experiences or with such happenings of his life and thus he will be impressed with such emotional experiences as will tend to relax or bring him into closer contact and harmony with the more vital and natural forces which are permeating his being. Thus he can undergo a tremendous emotional experience while witnessing an act or a play on the stage or that an orchestra can render a very beautiful rendition of some great masterpiece and he will be equally emotionally impressed.

In all cases, however, the fundamental science of vibronics which lies behind these things have to be thoroughly learned and impinged into the psychic consciousness of the composer or whoever brought this particular thing into expression. You simply do not take a lot of words and lump them together or a lot of notes and spread them about on paper and expect to get good results. That is not so. So here we will see hundreds, yes thousands of students who are learning the proper composition of tone forms or word pictures in their various constituents as wave train energies which have a very definite relationship not only to the nerve centers of the human but also to some of the physical centers of the body which are also actually a mass of nerve centers.

As we are walking about, your mind is continually impressed by what you might think are a strange conglomeration of bongs, pings, twangs and various other peculiar sounding notes which seem to come into your consciousness. You are also impressed by some other things which you have not yet learned to distinguish. Actually, these are word-form pictures and not expressed in the term of suggestive vowels and consonants of your language as it is used on the earth plane, but they are actual energies which have been projected into your consciousness from such sources, and these particular wave form trains are impressing a certain sequence of intelligence in your mind. In other words, it is merely another form of mental telepathy. In this case, the telepathic comm-union has as its source one or more of these various weird-looking electronic apparatuses which you see about you which the students are using to produce these various wave-train energies, so that by now you will begin to understand that it is not necessary to use the expressions of the vocal cords in resonating some kind of an intelligent thought pattern through the mentality of the individual.

You will see here also what appears to be some of the more familiar earth plane instruments which are used in the orchestra, such as the trumpets, and violins, the cellos, the woodwinds and the various other types of brasses and stringed instruments, yes, even the harps. Students here are also learning the usages and as to the proper production of certain wave train energies for which these instruments were primarily designed.

In passing over into this other section, you will be made aware that here are a number of instruments which are used in orchestras which are not of your earth plane but are in another plane of existence. You would be at a loss for words to describe these instruments, nor could we take the time in this transmission to do so. However, in each case of some physical or material plane, something similar to your earth, you will again find that in the existence of the race of mankind as it lives on that particular planet, all will express in their own way their innermost feelings through the various kinds of instruments which you will see about you.

In your jungles the savages are using the more primitive types of percussion instruments which are merely bones or drums, the bones or pieces of wood which are stretched across logs in a marimba-like fashion. And so starting with these more rudimentary forms of musical instruments, we can go on up and up into the tremendously advanced forms of instruments which are more purely electronic in nature. Some of these use the principles of reproduction of crystals. Others use the pure sine wave formations of electronic energy which are somewhat similar to the electronic organs of your earth plane.

Before I go too far in my transmission here today, the name William Shakespeare will no doubt conjure up one of the problems which has long confronted some of your fellow beings on the earth as to whether

or not I was once called Bacon or some other particular name. I will not attempt to clear up this mystery
and say yes or no at this time, but I will just say that
in my day and age at Stratford on Avon, at that time
it was very wise and very discreet for the person who
wished to express himself in a rather unorthodox
fashion, to do so under an assumed name. This would
help insure his safety. There were other things besides wood which were used for fuel for fires in those
days. In my time on your earth plane, it was not only
unlawful and illegal to think differently than those
above you, but it was also something which could be
extremely painful and very often resulted in death.

Now I believe it will be a very good place for us to
discontinue this particular transmission at this time.
I cannot say at this time whether I or one of my other
colleagues here will take over in the next transmission. However, we will try to make things as interesting as possible as you no doubt know by now that
this whole idea of the Shamballa is devoted to the
educational and scientific researches and expressions
of corrective therapies and such other associated
factors in the lives of the earth plane man. It is also
associated with teaching and with the proper inter-
polation of wisdom and knowledge into some of the
more numerous astral worlds which are in somewhat
of a lower rate of vibration than this particular center. In the near future, we shall take you to the astral
world of Muse where you will actually see how many
of these souls or personages who have lived on your
earth at different times are living and mingling with
the personages from other worlds who have also
lived in their own time in the physical body. This is
something of what has been called devachan or the
summerland or heaven. It merely means a place of
resting, reestablishing certain values or the working

out of certain particular types of spiritual karma before the proper place or step which will carry the individual soul into his next stage of evolution.

Not all of us come here to Parhelion as teachers or even as students. Many stop in these lower astral worlds and after some hundreds or even several thousands of years may again reincarnate from there into a lower physical plane. However, in due course of time, these points will be enlarged upon and explained to you if you have the patience and the time to write these things down. As it has been foretold, you will indeed possess much more knowledge and wisdom of these things than has previously ever been given to the earth plane and this is for the very important reason that the earth plane, as it is now known to you peoples about you, is going into a new state of evolution. It shall, as a planet and to the inhabitants who live upon that planet, evolve into a higher state of evolution and consciousness. The rocks, the earth, the trees, the animals, yes even the people who you see about you now will gradually through the centuries of time evolve into a higher dimension. Such as it is in the scheme of creation as it was conceived by the Infinite Intellect so all of these things must progress forward, even though they may be ever so slowly in your sense of time, yet surely they do so for this is the Infinite Plan. Until such further time, may God's peace be with you.

CHAPTER 40

I salute you, Brother and Sister on the earth plane. I am he who has been called Hilarion. Although there seems to be somewhat of a mystery attached to my identity, perhaps a few words would be in order at this point. I might say that I am not indigenous to your earth planet but have made evolutions in other planetary systems far removed from your solar system. I did, however, make two evolutions on your earth planet at two different times, one in Atlantis and one in India where I was known as Krishna. At present I am holding the position as the executive officer in this section of the city of Parhelion in the arts and sciences which are relative to the higher phases of culture in the earth plane as is so in many other of the similar planets in other solar systems.

It is only fitting that you be conducted through these various explorations, in the manner which is most befitting to you and one which will be of the greatest benefit and also one from which you will derive the greatest amount of personal gain in these explorations and visitations. It had originally been my purpose to meet you at the gate, however, as I am a member of the inner conclave of Patriarchs and Elders, I was unavoidably circumvented from making my appearance at this time, so I will beg your kindest indulgence. However, I do believe my colleagues Kung Fu and William gave a very good account of themselves in helping you to traverse our many halls and dimensions of learning here in the section of Muse. I see in your mind that you are still somewhat amazed and perplexed by the appearance of a high Avatar or rather, as we know him, as a Prince from one of the higher dimensions. He formerly held the position which I now occupy. He was Prince Serapis. No doubt many of your earth brothers and sisters will be greatly shocked just as you were at the appearance of a Celestial Being who had neither the arms nor legs or other of the rudimentary appearances of the physical body as you assume in your earth dimensional planes. However, you may rest assured that such appurtenances are entirely unnecessary in this highly elevated state of consciousness. We merely assume, shall I say, such physical appearances of such forms in these sections of Shamballa because we have not yet evolved, or shall I say to be more accurate, that it still serves a better purpose if we still maintain somewhat of a correct relationship with the lower earth or material orders of existence in these various planets.

Now that you have progressed so nicely through some of the settings here or the sections, there is still one remaining section which is actually the spoke part of the great wheel which stems from the central temple which you have not yet visited. So let us walk past the central fountain here which connects various corridors and enter into the spoke part itself. As was in the case of your former visitation in the more scientific part of the previous section which was devoted to science, this too is of immense size. Many floors or elevations with the central corridors are at least three or four hundred feet wide. In this case, however, as a museum it is devoted entirely to such exhibitions as are relative to our plane of expression. Thus you will find that up and down these corridors, you could stroll for many years and not see anything twice. You would find all types of things which relate to art, drama, to poetry, to literature, to sculpturing. You will see about you beautiful carved statues in all shapes and sizes made of strange and wonderful materials from foreign planets which you know nothing about. You will also see great cases in which reside all types of various other impedimenta which is relative to some artistic phase of life in some of these far-off planetary systems.

If you confine your observations to the earth plane perspective as it deals with your own planet, you will find the works of literally thousands of people who have formerly lived on your earth planet not to mention several thousand who are yet to make their reincarnation at some future date into that planet. As it was partly explained to you by William, your planet is now undergoing an evolution into a higher rate or a sphere of consciousness which will not only change the basic atomic structures of the earth itself but will also change such atomic structures in all living things on the earth in their relative position to the preceding dimensions or vortexes.

Now as we stroll casually down one of these corridors, I will attempt to elucidate and explain some of these things and cast a little more illumination into some of the darkened corners of your perspective so that your vision may assume somewhat of a lighter transparency. In other words, we will do our utmost to convey a clear picture not only to your own personal perspective, but to any and various sundry personalities who may read these lines. Our purpose here is to completely denude and to defraud any particular expression which has heretofore been given as to Shamballa. Your earth plane has long been confounded with a false preponderance of so-called esoterical values which have left the great masses of the population in a completely befuddled and be-muddled condition and by a natural consequence, it makes things increasingly difficult for we who are dedicated to the saving and the service of posterity to mankind to continually salve and to rehabilitate such personalities who have made wrecks of themselves by casting their own souls upon the rocks and shoals of a false religion.

Believe me, my friends, there is nothing artificial or superficial in your attitude or your belief of God. There is nothing which we will call esoterical or mystical. The processes which you are involved in on your earth plane shall fall away from you as a snake sheds its skin and thus it shall be, that you shall evolve through the countless eons of time and that you shall find the time or place that if you earnestly and conscientiously seek the answers to your problems that such answers will be given to you factually, without reservation and without malpractice. As my particular expression here in this section is devoted to literature, therefore I do have a little more of the vocabulistic entirety in my expression and for this I am quite thankful. It has long been my earnest desire and purpose working here to impart some of the wonderful knowledge and wisdom with which I am constantly surrounded in these beautiful centers here in Shamballa.

Now I see you have paused in front of some showcases. They look like some of the more familiar large glass cases that you might see in some of your earth museums with the exception, of course, that such structures are all constructed of the crystalline substances and all have their radiant transparent appearance. You are watching and seeing the small settings. These are actual stage presentations of many of the operas and plays such as William presented in his earth plane existence. These were all very cleverly contrived electrical and mechanical devices with miniature figures of men and women in actual stage settings in the various operatic scenes. By merely pressing this little button here, these particular figures will go through their acts clear to the entirety of the complete opera or the complete play, whichever the case may be. Also you will hear in your inward mental ear the entire libretto of such an opera or play. You will hear the beautiful cadent swelling of the female voices, the bassos, and also you will hear the tenors or various other male and female voices which are associated, not to mention orchestrations of the large symphonies which you see in the pits before these stages. These particular stage settings were, of course, all very cleverly constructed by the more scientific genius who resides in the section that you previously visited.

The purpose here, as they exist, is, of course, of educational value for the students who go through here from various other planets as well as your own earth plane to study such plays as "The Taming of the Shrew", or "The Merchant of Venice", or some particular opera by Verdi or Rossini or Ponchielli or any of the composers of such operas or operettas as have existed on the earth plane. The cases here are very numerous and would run into the hundreds of numbers. There are other very clever and wondrous devices which you will see from time to time as we walk slowly along here which depict somewhat in the nature or sense of such musical and artistic expression which exists in other planets in more or less of the same relative dimension as your earth plane. These, of course, will be strange and unfamiliar to you and would require a great deal of explanation which we

301

unfortunately do not have time for in this one particular book.

We would hope that if these efforts on our part are thus favorably received at this time and are not too premature that we may in the future enlarge with such counterparts as may seem necessary to further explain and elucidate such various facets.

As William explained to you, many of the people who have lived and attained some sort of an artistic expression, or as far as that goes, any other particular expression on your earth planes, do not all necessarily evolve into our centers of Shamballa. Many of these evolutions take many such earth-plane reincarnations before a person becomes even an Initiate. If I were also to take time to explain to you the various factors which enter into such personal counterparts of the numerous evolutions which exist in your own particular planet, I could devote many years in explaining as to who became who and so on through the ages of time which have existed on your earth plane.

To make a short and brief summary, let me say this, that anyone who has ever left anything to the posterity and benefit of mankind on your earth plane has had at some previous time several or a number of evolutions not only on your earth plane but on such similarly associated planes of existence on other planetary systems. These people are, in a large sense, free souls who are making somewhat of a series of progressions as Initiates. Later on they will become Adepts and so on into mastery as they master their various sciences with which they have associated themselves. But you may rest assured that if you see some outstanding personality on your earth plane in your present day, you may know that he came not through once but through many lifetimes into the position which he now occupies, not from your own earth plane but probably from many other planets. And as you spoke, even your Abraham Lincoln made his evolution from a black skin through the planet of Vulcan before he emerged as the president and emancipator of your colored race.

If you further desire a re-visitation of this gallery to study more of the arts and sciences at some future date, I will be most happy to be of service to you. It is my purpose, in our next visitation, however, to take you directly to the relative planet of Moose, or Muse as you call it, which is swinging off here in some other solar system other than your own. There you will visit many of the Initiates and Adepts who have, as I have spoken, made many evolutions through the various earth planes, such people as Madam Schumann-Heink, and others of such like nature, Enrico Caruso and many other of the great noted musical and operatic stars of the past, not to mention the poets, the various and sundry personalities who are too many and too numerous to mention. As William and Kung Fu said, "You have only to consult your own encyclopedia or almanac to obtain some sort of an idea about which I am speaking." So for the present time, let us rest with God's love.

CHAPTER 41

A cheery greeting to you, brothers and sisters, this is Iona. Just in case you have forgotten or do not immediately guess my presence, I will explain that I am the biocentric of Leonardo. Just in case this causes some surprise and my appearance here in Solferino, the central capital city of the planet of Muse, I may say that there is a definite reason for my appearing. As it so happens that the subject of biocentricity or the biune state of consciousness of mankind is of a particular interest to me. As a woman, you will appreciate my viewpoint and interest in, shall I say, my own sex. However, to put levity aside, we will go immediately into the business which is before us which is to further explain life as it exists in the higher realms and dimensions.

Now I believe you were left somewhere walking up the street of this wonderful and beautiful capital city, and that this is a very good place where we may start to further explain some of the various cycles and evolutions which have been undergone by those inhabitants of this very beautiful center. As you were further told, that all of these people are in themselves at least first or second degree Initiates, and in many cases they are Adepts in their particular expression of the inspirational arts of the lower astral worlds and the material planes of consciousness. No doubt you are wondering as you walk along the wide and beautiful thoroughfares which are lined with wonderful trees that seem to lace their branches overhead; you will notice that each dwelling place is a small estate all by itself and that it is surrounded by many acres of beautiful park-like grounds. The houses themselves are wonders of beauty and charm. I might tell you American housewives that there is none of the common so-called drudgery associated with the maintenance of these houses as there is no dish-washing, no dust to remove, no vacuuming or the various other things which you have associated with your homes on the earth planes. Such is the evolution of consciousness and concept that it will be so as you have constructed all of these things for yourself. Now you will wonder how this is done, so I will begin by explaining something more which may be somewhat repetitious in spots of the various evolutions which each individual is confronted with. As it was mentioned that starting in the lower material planes or worlds that men and women become various types of artisans and by that I mean that they may be carpenters or bricklayers or they may become plumbers or shoemakers. They may go into the various and innumerable crafts and sciences such as architecture, building railroads, bridges, skyscrapers and various innumerable things with which you have associated in your daily earth-plane existences.

Most of these men and women as individuals take a sort of fierce pride in their own craft or work, whatever it so consists of, so it is thus that they will continually for a number of reincarnations or evolutions so attach themselves to these material planes of expression. They will reincarnate and they will again become shoemakers or textile weavers or any one of the innumerable and numerous trades and professions which we could name at this time. Sooner or later, however, in these evolutions they will begin to be consciously aware of newer and higher dimensions. Such things as they are engaged in will be refined to a point that evolution and progress is only a matter of consequence and time, so in due course of these many evolutions they will find themselves in higher spiritual domains with the passing of each fleshy earth-plane life. As they have thus evolved into these higher dimensions, they will learn to so use and to so construct their knowledge with the materials and with the knowledge at hand. Instead of the brick-layer or the carpenter who is evolving into the lower astral plane, he will still continue his trade. He will cut wood or lay brick and will in consequence assume some new and different perspective of his craft or trade. So in the innumerable centuries and evolutions, he will finally arrive into such a dimension as is filled with the radiant energies as you see around you in this one particular planet which is somewhat similar to many of the other higher astral realms as well as the other centers of Shamballa.

So such artisans who have been the various crafts-men and tradesmen of the lower physical or material dimensions are now learning to use their skill and knowledge in an entirely new and different way. They thus learn to take the radiant energies as it sur-rounds them in these higher realms and dimensions and using it with other constructive energies such as are at hand at the present moment, construct the various and necessary things which are many of the beautiful crystalline structures which you see around you, the beautiful cities just as they were in Venus and in Parhelion. Much of this work has been done by these craftsmen who have evolved into these high-er dimensions.

Now no doubt in your earth plane you have seen men who took sand and gravel and with the addition of Portland cement and water, mixed it together and formed concrete; such was a basic building material in your earth plane structures. Here in these higher spiritual realms, some such a similar process is followed except here instead of using the sand and gravel, we use the radiant energies which are stemming from these great vortexes. The Portland cement is the mind energies which have stemmed from the various minds of the constructively minded individuals who are residing in the earth-plane consciousness.

You have been told that the power of prayer if it is properly directed is of such nature that it can be properly used for the purposes of spiritual therapy and healing. So likewise are the energies which stem from the minds of those who are constructively employed. We say that the artist who is painting a beautiful picture or the doctor who is performing a piece of surgery and that his complete mind is focused in an attempt to heal and save the life of his patient or we might say that those who are thus employed in the more constructive phases of your civilization such as it is around you, they are not only performing their various functions in a rather, momentarily at least, detached and unselfish perspective of attitude, but they are primarily interested and concentrating in a direction of performing some service to their fellowman. There are many of these higher types of mentally developed people around you who have in their minds the more spiritually evolved principles which activate such trades or crafts in which they are employed.

As Jesus once said, "Lay ye not treasures on earth but rather, lay ye up treasures in heaven." You will, of course, wonder how it would be that a person could lay up treasures in heaven when heaven seemed to be such a remote and a far-off place, but the treasures of which He spoke were these mind energies which were focused in constructive and spiritual channels in your daily lives. Such energies, in ascending to these higher realms of consciousness, are taken in hand or rather in mind by those who know of the secrets of combining these various energy forces. They are thus projected into the crystalline structures of the cities and of the other wonderful and magnificent things which you see about you. Now I believe that this will somewhat explain to you why it is that such people may arrive into these dimensions and find that they already have some such beautiful home in which it is just a matter of almost moving into. You have somewhat of a concept in the earth plane which has been rather badgered around from time to time which says that when you die you go to heaven, ride around on a pink cloud and play a harp. Now this planet is pink in its general, shall I say, overlaying color vibration yet as you look about you, the grass is just as green as it has been in any of the other places where you have been. The trees are just as beautiful and symmetrically shaped and of just as much abundance and variety as any place. The flowers here are blooming in a lush profusion just as they do in many of these higher spiritually evolved planes. Everything seems to be so well ordered and so well kept. This is, of course, due to the fact that a constant and a terrific amount of mental energy is projected into the maintenance and keeping of these things in such condition.

When I said, "All play and no work," that it was such, the people who live in these various places are putting forth daily not the fun or frivolity or the things which you might think but they are doing a considerable and a great deal of mental work which is so constructively directed that it not only helps other planes, dimensions and the people living there but that it also helps to keep their own cities and their own planets in a beautiful state of vibration.

Now as I said before, this is a particularly good place in which the fullest measure of the biocentric concept can be entered into. As we walk down these various thoroughfares before we emerge into the central part of the city, I will point out to you various dwelling places of the earth-plane personalities who have lived in your more recent times. I am doing this to carry the full impact of what we mean when we say marriages or soul mates of the higher astral realms as well as these particular centers of Shamballa.

I would like you to stop here and pause a moment and look back into the pathway where there is a very wonderful and beautiful dwelling place. Like all the others that are constructed here, and that you see before you, this too is of almost a transparent crystalline structure. The walls sweep around in very graceful lines; the roof is overlaid in a very bright coral shade and all about the house is an air of extreme simplicity and charm. This happens to be the home of one you called at your earth-plane existence, Mark Twain, or as he is rightly known, Samuel Clemens. He was one of the fortunate individuals who found his soul mate in the earth plane and lived with her during his earth life so that he and she are here living in their spiritual simplicity which they rightfully earned through their many evolutions.

Here again as we walk farther along this thoroughfare, we will see another very beautiful dwelling place in which the general scheme seems to be something of a more blue cast. However, the color is immaterial. This is the home of one who has somewhat collaborated with you in the field of poetry. His name is Walt Whitman. You know of him in his earth life as he wandered up and down the fair land of America and that he visited many other countries and climes in the earth world and that he left behind him a great wealth and treasure of very beautiful poetry, yet he did not know the comfort and security, the warmth and spiritual love of his biune counterpart. This was one of the factors which entered in which made him such a restless soul and which gave such a tremendous spiritual impetus to his work. Now, however, he is living here quietly with his biocentric mate just as the others do in their full spiritual consciousness and light.

Over there on the corner is the home of Robert and Clara Schumann. They were in the musical world sometime about ninety or a hundred years ago on your earth plane. Robert and Clara had a rather tempestuous life before they became wedded and even after they were wed they did not know a complete continuity or a spiritual consciousness of their love but only for rather brief interludes because of the nature of their work, as they were both in the musical world thus it was that their careers often kept them separated as well as various other things such as family clashes. However, here they have worked out and completed and have fulfilled to its entirety their biocentric consciousness.

Now as we turn down around here is a little lane which leads off down into a byway by the side of a small trickling stream of water. That is the home of one who lived on your earth plane known as Franz Schubert. He was the unfortunate young man who passed away at about the age of thirty-two and knew not the comfort and spiritual security of his biocentric companion. Here, however, his full destiny is complete. She is united with him as she waited for him in one of the other astral worlds until he was again able to rejoin her. I could go on and on and point out other and innumerable examples of such nature which read like the most fantastic and romantic love stories that you have ever read or seen composed on your earth plane. Yes indeed, these cities have been not only the scene of many joyful reunions but they have also been scenes of somewhat saddened partings wherein someone who had gained and worked his or her way into such a perspective field of knowledge that it was imperative for the person to leave and to reincarnate into a lower earth plane. Thus it was that their biocentric would also leave their beautiful and charming residence and also go somewhere to participate in such activities.

There is a story about Nicola, or Nicholas Tesla, and that it is in the biography as it was printed in one of the earth-plane books. However, it is a very beautiful and touching story and one which bears repeating. Tesla never knew the warmth and security of his biocentric mate on the earth plane but she was able to come to him in the form of a beautiful white dove. Thus it was through the years of his earth plane existence that she frequently made her appearance in a materialized condition in the form of this beautiful white dove, where she would circle about and light upon his shoulder and after cooing a few moments, she would disappear. At one time in the latter part of Tesla's life as he was sitting contemplating on some of the inner mysteries, this beautiful white dove or his soul mate, entered into the open window fluttered upon his shoulder and fell dead at his feet. Some way through, shall I say, a short circuit, the connection was broken and so it was that a few years later, Tesla too left his physical body and rejoined his mate in their domain. Tesla and his biocentric are now residing in the scientific center of Shamballa.

And so, dear ones, remember you are living in an age which is a fulfillment of the prophecies in more ways than one. Even in the construction of your houses as you see them and that they are composed largely of large surfaces of glass, so they are beginning to take on the face of these more celestial mansions which you are looking about and seeing at the present moment. You are also seeing various and other manifestations. Your own government has some very outstanding examples which have not been repeated in the histories of time of your earth plane. The leaders of your nation have been united together. Those who you call Ike and Mamie are indeed soul mates, so are the Nixons, the Warrens and so are the Knights. There are others in your earth plane too who are bio-centrics and have been so fortunate as to be united with themselves at that crucial moment and hour in the history of the earth, for indeed the earth is in a crucial and critical period of its progression.

Only in the combined spiritual forces, which are stemming from the united and concerted efforts of the earth people as they live in your advanced and beautiful America, can you hope to turn back the tides of the black and evil astral worlds which are swarming about you. You have read much about the battle of Armageddon yet surely, for the past seven or eight years, you have been fighting the battle of Armageddon. You have called it a cold war but surely it is as it has been prophesied, the red mists from the East have been swirling about you, and only by your spiritual efforts, your united cooperation not only with yourselves and your loved ones but with the higher forces from the realms of Shamballa, can you ever hope to overcome these swirling red and black mists which are about you.

So, loved ones, think much about the things which

312

have been revealed to you. Love your neighbor as yourself and love your God with all your heart and your soul. Work constructively and with the full knowledge and consciousness that your efforts shall and will be richly rewarded, for surely these things are the treasures in heaven.

As you go forward in your various evolutions and reincarnations, never cease to have the patience and forbearance which will help you to overcome the trials and tribulations and vicissitudes which come your way. Always in whatever hour of need as well as in those moments in which you are fully thankful and aware, will you continually seek out the help and aid and the assistance of those who have been assigned the special duties of helping you in your reincarnations in the earth planes. Each one of you in your material realms have your own guardian angel, an angel who comes to you from one of the angelic kingdoms. You have also other forces which are more relative to the working out of problems and while your guardian angel is of the directional or inspirational nature, yet surely there must be others who will help you in such fundamental and corrective therapies with which your daily lives must be properly constituted and interwoven. And so my brothers and sisters, in full humbleness and in full thankfulness, I have come to you in some such small capacity as is so.

On our next visitation, we will continue on into this beautiful city of Solferino (Coralanthea) and we will examine just exactly its fullest and innermost nature and in the capacity, as it does, of teaching many of the lower astral and earth plane realms in the various five inspirational sciences. But until such time, we send you the fullest measure of our love.

313

CHAPTER 42

Good morning, dear ones. We are the Brownings. I am Elizabeth and Robert is here beside me. It was thought apropos at this time by Iona and others that as our story is somewhat well known to you people on the earth, that we should conduct you in our next tour into our fair city of Coralanthea. Robert has insisted that I do all the talking so if you do not hear from him, he will be here nevertheless. We have not yet arrived back into the immediate vicinity of the orb of Muse so now we shall take a little astral flight. The purpose here was to enable you to obtain something of a bird's eye view of this fair and beautiful place before we descended properly within the city limits. There is a particular ceremony which is going to be taking place a little later on. There are a group of plebeians from the lower astral planes and from several of the sub-planets which are going to go through the ceremony of initiation so that they may become full-fledged neophytes in our fair city.

But see, now we have arrived somewhere at a point where we can obtain a panoramic view of the vista before us. In the far distance you are seeing two very beautiful peaks. There is a story from the earth that we are familiar with of the twin peaks of Copernicus which stood above the city of Athens in Greece. These twin peaks are somewhat similar in shape to the much publicized mountain of Fujiyama in Japan, except that they are very beautiful crystal structures which seem to glow with all of the iridescent beauty of the rainbow. At the base of these beautiful peaks is the city of Coralanthea. Just in case you are a bit confused with the difference in names to one which was given you previously, I might say that this city is known by several different names in different planetary systems. However as William once said, "A rose by any other name would be just as sweet;" so we will continue with our exploration.

Stretching out over the plain in front of these two beautiful peaks for a hundred miles in each direction, you will see the various dwellings and centers which comprise the city. It stretches out in somewhat of a fanlike fashion. If you remember the old-fashioned fans the ladies used to use at the balls and social functions many years ago, that they were composed of beautiful ostrich plumes or of some such similar material. We might say that these streets and cities converge down in a fanlike fashion toward the central hub which is actually a large group of buildings. We are not confined or cramped for space in this fair city and as you saw by a previous exploration on the surface, that all of the dwellings are in themselves small estates or parks. And that is the reason why so much teritory is covered, because everyone here insists on having plenty of room, and well it is so.

As we are getting somewhat closer to the central part of the city, we can see that it is something which we might compare to a half section of a pie and that we divide this half section of a pie into five equal slices. Each one of these portions of the pie is a representation or functions as its own center of learning and teaching in each of the five inspirational arts as they have been classified for you. The buildings themselves are something like about twenty or twenty-five miles long with a diameter which is equally divided among themselves so you see that they are quite a vast and large size. They are also many storied and tower into the air which would compare with some of the larger buildings in your earth cities. At the very apex or center of this half section, there is a huge temple which will remind you somewhat of the temple you saw in Parhelion. This, too, is also of a very vast and large size although it is not as large as the one in that particular city. So let us make a landing here, as it were, and we will walk on up one of the streets which divides these sections. A little later on we will come back into one of these sections and explore more fully just what it is that takes place and what the particular functions are within these various sections. But now the time has almost arrived for the initiation ceremony.

As you will see as we approach the temple, there are three different tiers of steps and that each tier is composed of three steps, then there is a landing, then there are three more steps and so on. There are also five different entrances which are spaced equally around the outside diameter or periphery of the face of the temple. Each one, of course, corresponds to its own section or center.

We shall enter the center section which is nearest to us and as we do so, we will see that there is a difference here in this temple with the one we saw in Parhelion inasmuch as it is much more like a large theater of your earth plane. At the extreme rear of this huge temple is an enormous stage with a great canopy or dome-like structure over the top. At the apex of this dome are huge crystals and prisms and just as in the case of other temples you have seen, these are used for purposes of focusing energy beams from the outside dimensions into the theater. Such are the functions of these crystals that they can thus bring the energies into a fuller and a more utilitarian purpose. In looking about you, you will see that this huge temple or theater is already filled and that it looks something like the great metropolitan opera house in one of your earth plane cities except that here everything is constructed in a beautiful stream-lined manner with great balconies which are over-hanging each other and extend on and on up into the huge dome-like overhead structure. As you can see it can very easily house several hundred thousand souls. Down on the center of the stage, you will see a rather elongated cube which is actually composed of three different stages or elevations. The bottom layer is of a red structure and about a foot high, the second one is yellow and the third is blue. They are sitting one upon each other something like layers on a cake. Each layer is somewhat smaller than the other, so that it forms a step. At the rear of this great stage, a group of people are standing. These are the leaders of the various sections as they are standing waiting for the proper moment when the initiation takes place.

Now that we are comfortably seated, we will see that it is about to begin. As we wait expectantly for a moment, then there is a sort of a sing-song chant which you have begun to be familiar with except that in this case it seems to be more like the more familiar choruses that you have heard the large groups give in stage presentations on your earth plane. It is something reminiscent of Handel's "Chorus of Elijah". You can hear the music swelling and diminishing in a great cascade and torrent of sound within your mind and as you look about you, you do not see the lips or any of the facial features of the people here moving, yet within their mind is the swelling cadence of this enormous chorus. Now looking at the stage, you are again seeing something which is very fantastically beautiful. From the three prisms and the lenses above the stage are focused three beams of energy which converge upon the center of the elongated cubes. There is a long red beam, then there is a beautiful golden beam and there is a very intense blue beam. As these beams are focused like spot-lights, you will see that at the base of these beams there begins to grow something like a dancing, pulsating flame of energy. Slowly these flames grow until they are about the height of ten feet. They have the appearance of a fountain cascading and pulsating in a very beautiful display of iridescent colors. They, however, maintain the overall primary radiance as we first mentioned, the first is red, the second is yellow and the third is blue.

Now everything seems to be in order. The music has swelled to a very loud and tremendous volume. Now from one side of the stage, there is formed a long line of a group of people. They are all dressed in very simple, white flowing tunics. They are the plebeians who are about to take the initiation ceremony. Slowly as the music begins a chant-like rhythm, keeping in step and in harmony with this chant, they walk toward the stage. As they pass by the stage each one pauses momentarily beside a pedestal upon which is placed a very large thick book. As they pause momentarily, keeping in time and rhythm with the chant, they place their left hand upon the book and place the tips of their right fingers on their forehead, then they raise their right hand and pass on, each one doing the same particular gestures. These gestures are tokens or pledges of complete fidelity.

Now you will see that the first of these plebeians has approached the base of the three steps which lead up to the first of the red flames. Slowly he begins taking one step at a time, keeping in rhythm with the music. At the top he does not even pause but walks directly into the red flame and with the next step he emerges from the other side and so on; he will pass from the red into the golden and then into the blue. As you will see, as all persons walk through the flame and then emerge, they have taken on something of the color of the flame, and so by the end of the procession where they have passed through the three flames, they have taken on all three of these primary basic radiations; so that now instead of the white or drab appearance which they first had in entering the flames, they are now like the rest of us around here and they are pulsating in the full radiance of the colors. Slowly the chant-like music continues until the last of this group has passed through. There have been about twenty-five who have taken this initiation ceremony. They have come, as I have said, from the sub-planets and the higher astral realms of your earth plane.

It might be a note of interest to say that several of them quite recently lived on your earth plane. However, they were not generally or well-known in the sense of the word and so I will not mention their names at this time. Now that the ceremony has been completed and they are all now neophytes living here among us, we will take ourselves out of the temple so that we may visit one of the centers which is devoted to its own particular function that we may best examine and see just what is the nature of the things which are taking place.

As it was first previously described, it is a large, somewhat of a wedge-shaped building which is perhaps about 20 miles long and as high as a fairly high skyscraper or building. There are a number of levels or floors. The whole building, just as the other four, are constructed of a beautiful crystal-like substance, very translucent, with an overall pervading radiance which is something of a pink or coral cast and such is the name we have taken for the city, which is Coralanthea. As we enter into the base part of this huge building, this one happens to be devoted to the inspirational art of literature. As we pass through the large entrance into the central corridor, we will walk down this corridor and will see that on each side, just as in the case of some of the other large buildings we have visited that there are various kinds of classrooms.

We will go into one of these classrooms and see just what is taking place. As this section is devoted to the art of literature, we will therefore see that all duties and activities are more or less confined along the lines of composition as it is done in the earth plane such as relates to story writing, whether it is fictional or whether it is of a true nature, also such things as history, autobiographies and other and numerous phases and branches of the literary arts. As we emerge into this classroom, you are quite surprised to see that it is a very beautiful place, something like the classrooms which you saw on Parhelion. Here is a vast and a beautiful expanse which stretches out before you and while there are a great deal of beautiful plants, shrubs and trees which are growing around on the outside yet the center itself seems to be rather like a huge theater.

In front of the sphere through the several thousand seats which are immediately in front of this theater are seated and filled with a large group of children. These children seem to range in age from about eight years to about twelve years old. These children happen to be all from your own earth plane. As it is night-time there and about two o'clock in the morning, these children are here in their astral consciousness. I believe that this way of teaching was explained to you in your visitation on the planet of Venus and it is carried on in the same fashion here, except of course that we do not teach the spiritual arts but rather, we teach the inspirational arts as they relate to music and art, drama, literature and sculpturing. You might be surprised to learn that the instructor who is teaching this group of children and telling them a story and teaching them in the various arts of story telling is one who was known on your earth plane as Aesop. I believe he gave quite a lengthy volume of some stories which were called Aesop's Fables and still exist in the classrooms of your earth plane schools.

Now we can pass from this center and go into other centers where you will see adults being taught the higher forms of composition and rhetoric. We can also see other functions which relate to public speaking or elocution and such other sundry and kindred things which are of the same nature. So, all in all, we can say that this section here is a vastly large and expanded college or university wherein the very highest phases and forms and technical aspects of composition in various languages and in various earth plane dimensions are here taught. Such scholars come from various planets in the galaxy of star clusters to which we are related and come across the vast distances of what is called space. They may live here outside in the city or they may actually come and go in different periods of time in their various existences.

Later on, many of these students will, of course complete their courses and graduate. They may thus become teachers and students in the higher centers of Parhelion or they may again reincarnate into some earth plane to begin a teaching career or some such

321

career which will give them full expression of the art which they have somewhat fully learned in these particular sections.

Now let us pass from this section and go into the next one. Walking across the large central passageway, we again emerge into another section which is devoted to the inspirational science of drama, as it is called on the earth plane. What this means is the factual presentation of the various and innumerable concepts in people's lives as they are depicted in such plays or pageantry with which you are more or less familiar. All types of drama and presentations and pageantry are taught in these classrooms. It might be of interest to the people of Southern California to know that their own Rose Parade had its origin and was under the direct supervision of a group of students and graduates from this particular section. It was formerly instigated as a direct inspiration from this group of students and is thus carried on from year to year in an inspirational manner from this plane or dimension. So likewise we may say in a more or less relative sense or degree that other such ceremonies, observances and pageantry on your earth plane as well as many others are likewise of such inspirational nature that they are in some way linked and expressed through these centers here in Coralanthea.

As you will see, just as in the previous section that large groups of small and large children from the various planets in the different solar systems are here taught in their astral moments when they are asleep. So it is that many of these youngsters soon express a high degree of precocity in some relative dramatic art. This may somewhat account for many of the appearances of these infant prodigies, such as violinists or dancers in the various types of terpsichore, of ballet or other similar and kindred stage presentations. I would like to point out here that we do not teach some of the lower forms of music and dancing as it is expressed on your earth plane at this particular time. You have many forms of, shall I say, degenerative types of dancing which is called jitterbugging. There are also some types of music which are called bebop or jive which is also of a degenerative nature. We do not teach anything here of such an inharmonious nature, in which would give rise to various inharmonic chords or discontents within one's nature. Such phases of music and dancing have their origin in the lower astral realms and come primarily from the forces which have passed over into spirit and which are malcontents or, as you sometimes refer to them, as dark forces. Our expressions in these various centers as they are taught in the inspirational arts are properly correlated with the innermost nature of man which has its infinite origin and as its source the great Fountainhead which is sometimes referred to as the Creator or God.

Now Robert and I would wish that you rest for a while and we will take up very shortly at this point and where we will leave off, so may you rest in peace until we see you in a little while.

CHAPTER 43

Greetings of the new day to you, brother and sister. I see you are standing before a case in this great central library hall of our section of Parhelion and that you are very much engrossed in watching the tiny figurines as they are enacting their various dances. The one you are looking at, as I see, is Tschaikovsky's Swan Lake Ballet but come, there are more wondrous things for you to see. Now as we walk along beside these many cases, here are others which would be of tremendous interest to you had you the time to witness them. Here is a scene from Verdi's Aida; here is also Rigoletto. Puccini's Madame Butterfly is portrayed in the next case. Here is a particularly beautiful rendition of Wagner's Tristan and Isolde and so on. Of course, all of the operas which have been written and produced on your earth plane are not exactly portrayed in these cases, just those which are of particular interest and which have, shall I say, a sense of immortality in their creation. In the lower centers you will find other such portrayals done not only with mechanical figurines but also in real life presentations very similar to those you have witnessed on your earth plane.

Now that we have come up into the section of the library which is devoted to the storage of books, you are looking with wonder and amazement at the tremendous size and height of these various cases which contain the innumerable volumes which have been produced on the hundreds and even thousands of earth planes. Here too all of the literature which is so produced on those earth planes is stored here. In this case, it is only that literature which has been produced by the Initiates or the Adepts or other highly intellectually and spiritually motivated forces. As you will note, the ceiling extends above you to something like a height of several hundred feet and that the cases are innumerable and extend down into the distance which is actually very many miles long. These cases store many millions of books which have been written by the many hundreds of thousands of authors who have been connected with these various earth plane experiences. I see there are many questions which are pouring from your mind but first let us examine one of the books. You will reach into this nearest case and as you see, these are all small cases which are divided into shelves which extend on and on into the distances around you.

Now you have taken hold of one particular volume which is very much unlike the volumes which you find in your public libraries. It is only like them in one respect that it has a cover and some pages inside. However, here the similarity ends. The particular book you have happens to be taken from the case which has been devoted to the stories of works by Robert and Elizabeth Browning. As you will note, the cover of this book is not like the covers of the books on your earth plane but it is of a very particularly beautiful plastic-like material which is luminous and iridescent in color. This is because of the very high inspirational value of the poetry which is contained therein. Now if you will open the pages here, you will also see some very marked differences from the volumes in your earth plane libraries. The volume itself is about one-third the size of any volumes you might expect to see of such a nature and the pages themselves are also of some material which you do not recognize immediately. It seems to be a sheet of very fine, thin, energy-like material which it actually is. It is not paper in the sense of the word that you would confine paper as a manufactured product on your earth plane. This is a pure form of energy which has been brought into use through mind force. The writings themselves, as you will see, are tiny miniature reproductions of not the commonly accepted vocabulary of earth-plane forms but in this case, they are definite spiritual symbols. If you are properly tuned to these symbols, you will see that they will convey to you not the idea of thought form as it is expressed in a chain of word sequences but expresses to you the entire idea of what the person who was so writing this book was inspired by at that particular moment.

Thus it is with all of the books in this particular great section or library section of this city. I see you are also wondering as to how these books were written and how they are cataloged and various other factors which you might think relative. As in the case of the Brownings, that in writing these books as do all of the authors or composers, they all impinge, shall I say, their own particular rate of vibration. No cataloging system is necessary but any student who goes through these corridors and who wishes to contact the books of Tennyson or Keats or any of the authors who have been on your earth plane merely thinks of them and immediately he is there by the case. It is as simple as that. He has merely to select the proper volume, hold it in his hands and he will immediately be in tune and in contact with the particular inspiration which created that book.

As to the actual construction of the books themselves, this has been largely done by the Initiates or Adepts before they ever emerged into your earth plane. Thus you will easily see how it was possible for Handel to begin composing music at the tender age of seven and Mendelssohn had already composed symphonies before he was fourteen. These things were merely brought into expression by these Initiates from books which they had previously composed in such centers which are similar to the one which you are in.

And so it is not only in the fields of literature, art and various other of the more highly evolved forms of spiritual inspiration in man's nature but also into the more relative fields of science and of the more materialistic natures. In most cases and generally speaking, a large part of such production in earth planes is usually brought into expression from the original plane in which the Initiate or the Adept emerged from into the earth plane consciousness. Now we could wander up and down these various corridors where these millions of volumes are stored and that we could select at random any one of the hundreds of various literary components of expressionists on your earth plane. We could contact anyone of the more philosophical nature as well as those in poetry and literature. We find here volumes which deal with almost every relative concept of life. However, as I have previously explained, this section is devoted primarily to the arts of literature and their various and kindred and associated sciences, music, poetry, sculpturing and painting.

Now let us emerge into another section. Here you will see that the walls and the various partitions are devoted to the art of painting. Here again you will see in such miniature forms as well as in full life size, expressions of the various artists who have lived on your earth plane. Here you will be in contact with such notables as Van Dyck, Michelangelo, Titian, yes even Leonardo has one of his masterpieces hung in one of these galleries even though he is the head executive of the scientific section of Parhelion.

Also in various corridors you will find the works which have been done in the art of stone or in marble which has been termed sculpturing. This work also is done in such other and sundry associated materials which will be found on the various earth planes. Wood, jasper, onyx and a host of other materials which were native to each particular planet are used to carve the various configurations either in the human form or in such symbology as may express the particular inspirational value of the Initiate or Adept who has worked so constructing these things.

You are also no doubt wondering at the vast amount of material which is produced in the field of literature on your earth plane as well as in various other fields which is not, shall I say, of superior nature. If we think for a moment that as we have only stored here such things as are of a very high spiritual nature that there must be indeed and there is a great deal of such material which is of a salacious nature and is not conducive to the highest rate of intelligence. This material is, of course, stored in its relative form in various centers which are revolving in the lower orders of frequency relationships down through the lower astral planes. Thus it is that you will find if you could go far enough that the so-called black forces also have libraries where they store much of this salacious or sadistic material which is relative to their particular plane of existence. They include a vast amount of books which deal primarily with the material issues of life on your earth plane such as the exploitation of sex and various other factors, heinous crimes of murder and violence in which magazines and books have been written in the nature of these things. Here too you will find in these lower orders of astral realms such vast storehouses of this material. They are in turn reproduced by, shall I say, initiates who emerge into the earth plane from these lower orders. You will be surprised that there are initiates from these dark regions who emerge into your earth plane but such is the case.

Your own Adolph Hitler was one of these and I will say he was not an initiate but was an adept. You have other shining and striking examples, if I can use the term shining rather loosely. We might say that the Genghis Khan and other of the great butchers who have bloodied the pages of your history have been products of these lower astral regions and they were adepts and masters in their own arts. However, I wish to avoid confusion at this time so I will not go farther into these relative factors other than to merely suggest that their existence is very real and that in consequence, all earth people should thus wisely heed these words and in being cognizant of such relative factors as can be expressed in their daily earth plane lives and existences; they should be made fully aware of these things in such a positive stance or reactionary way that they can obtain some measure of protection from these lower astral forces.

In the past much has been written as to purgatory, Hades and other places where the so-called wicked or the dead are supposed to be incarcerated. These things are, of course, largely fictional in value. However, the idea or form from which they sprang is indeed very real. One of the works which is stored here (in this center of Parhelion) comes from an Italian by the name of Dante who wrote the familiar "Inferno". In this he produced a very real example of such ideology as could be expressed in the metaphor of the mental or the spiritual capacity of such people who have gone on into the astral worlds without sufficient knowledge and learning of the spiritual values of life. Thus it is that they wander in these Hades-like formations of thought patterns until the day of liberation comes, not from without but from within their own minds and their own thinking.

A little later on we shall actually go to the planet Muse upon the Ray Beam and there you will see very accurate real-life presentations of the various operas, festivals, and plays which have been produced on your earth plane as there are many people there who are Initiates who produce much and very beautiful works which are relative to your higher spiritual values of life. This museum section of the spoke which we have just partially completed exploring, as I have said, is many miles long and our one particular difficulty here is in expressing even a very small fraction of the gigantic nature of the project which we have undertaken in creating this in the book form for the earth peoples to read. However, I believe that this will be sufficient for general purposes that you may gain somewhat of an idea. And so for this particular transmission, may I wish you the most pleasant and abundant of God's munificent blessings.

CHAPTER 44

Our most hearty welcome to you, brother and sister, and we are indeed very happy that you are here with us again in our fair city. I see that I have found you wandering about in the very large section of our museum which is devoted to painting and art. I see that you are admiring some of the paintings by some of the Italian artists. That one hanging there in particular is very beautiful and one that has been done by Botticelli. There is also another one here by the side which is a Cellini. We could go up and down this particular corridor which is devoted to this type of Italian art of the Renaissance which has its own particular flavor and appeal.

During the preceding hours I have received some buzzing in my ears and I knew that you were thinking about some very pertinent problems or questions which perhaps it might be well that we cleared up before we continued our visitation into such other centers as are in the immediate future. These questions are pertaining to such things as the much-bandied concept of reading the Akashic records, initiations, and so on and so forth. I will open our little discussion by saying that very little if any of the more highly evolved concepts which relate to the more progressive states of man's mental attitudes in the earth plane are of spontaneous origin. As it was previously pointed out, man is very seldom, if ever, truly constructive in his line of thought. Such thinking principles are usually derivations of preordained or, shall I say, preconceived thought patterns and ideologies or philosophies which had their origin in spiritual planes of consciousness which were relative to man's earth-plane existence and one in which he previously existed at some other time. The Yogis have a word on your earth plane which they call the Akashic. This in a simple sense of the word merely means the life record of some particular individual whether it concerns him in his present earth life or in some previous reincarnation. Now to the materialist as he exists in the earth plane, such things as are apt to be found in other dimensions which are immediately relative to his senses of perception in his present state of consciousness would be utterly impossible for him to conceive. In spite of the fact that he has a very good memory and could remember things back to his childhood, yet such intangible things other than his memory consciousness seem to have escaped him at the moment. However, we will not deal with such materialistic values at this present moment, rather we shall deal with personages or personalities who have gone somewhat beyond this materialistic realm of expression and, shall we say, have become slightly, or more so, clairvoyant or psychic. In discussing our terminology of initiation here, I shall not refer to the more highly evolved orders of initiation which takes place in the higher spiritual planes of consciousness. Such things would be out of place to be given to the earth people or even to yourself at this present moment. Such things are properly realized and participated in only in their relative states of consciousness in your own evolutions.

We shall begin with a general summation by

starting the progress of any one particular individual in some lower order of materialistic earth plane existence. He is in such a state of divided consciousness between the carnal and physical natures of his self and of such innate or, into the present time at least, the spiritual desires of his inner nature have been suppressed. In such a carnal or materialistic state of life, he will revolve about into such earth plane expressions for a seemingly endless number of such reincarnations until such time as it occurs to him that there may be other things in life besides food, sex, sleep and other things of these materialistic values. He may come in contact with people who are expressing a higher spiritual concept in life and some of these spiritual values may permeate into the more darkened regions of his mind. He may become infused somewhat with a desire to express himself in a more spiritual or a more fully evolved and developed nature than he has heretofore displayed. This will, of course, be his first step or his first initiation. This is born out of his relative desires of his spiritual nature to elevate himself from his lustful purposes of his many earth lives.

Now he will find himself in a position where whole new worlds will open up before him. He will find that as he looks about him and seeks help that he will find help. He will find new avenues which will open up for him which will lead him into pathways which have heretofore been closed and inaccessible. He will find that he will revolve into different spiritual worlds with the passing of each earth-plane existence; he will revolve and will reincarnate into higher spiritual planes and in such planes he will lay down some pattern which he will follow in each succeeding reincarnation in some lower domain.

Now there is a very important point that we must

remember here. As I have said, nothing of any relative importance has been brought into existence on the earth-plane dimension which has not been previously conceived or preconceived in some such spiritual dimension, previous to the time of such individual's appearance in the earth plane expression, and in such time as he brought forth whatever particular thing it was that he excelled in or that he was able to bring about for the purposes of the benefit of his fellow-man. In a more scientific approach to viewing this all-important equation lies simply in the fact of under-standing the true spiritual nature of man, the inward self. As has been explained to you, this consists of the linkage which is called the psychic body. Now as you know and you have been told, this consists of count-less millions of tiny wave form vortexes which are all the intelligent quotients and elements which have entered into the individual's various reincarnations, earth lives and spiritual planes of development.

It is easy to see if we think for one moment that the coarser or the more carnal and lustful vibrations which were conceived in the lower earth plane dimen-sions were of such nature that they had no true mo-tivating power or no true God-Force in their construc-tion, as they were conceived without the full coopera-tion and the entirety of the spiritual counterpart of the individual. So it must be that in the full light of the newer realization and consciousness, such lower elemental wave form thought patterns as existed in these psychic bodies would be neutralized or rectified or would, for lack of sustenance, pass and disappear from the psychic body and thus be replaced with the higher and more refined of the wave form conscious-nesses of the new spiritual developments. And thus it would be with each succeeding evolution through some higher and higher spiritual plane of relative consciousness, that the individual would constantly replace and impinge into his psychic body the newer and the more refined and the more spiritually composed wave forms which were in consequence, much more imperishable in nature.

The end result, as it has been explained to you, would completely obliterate all such physical traits of consciousness of each individual and make him a pure Infinite Creation which was of the sublime God Force in its entirety, such a person as you saw speaking from the rock in the center of the lake in a previous transmission.

But getting back to reading the Akashic, as it is called in the earth plane, and it is a much bandied phrase and little understood. I might say right here that there are very few, if any, of your earth people who can truly read the Akashic records. Such clairvoyants or psychics as are in existence in your earth plane are not of an advanced nature in their concepts that they can peer back into the hundreds or the thousands of years in the preceding lives of any such individuals. I say that there are a few, but such individuals do not entirely know to a large extent just exactly how these processes are brought about, so I would like to point out that there is a certain combination of circumstances which must be brought into focus before such true revelations can be brought into existence or the focuses of attention and thus viewed introspectively in the full values and light for which they are brought into existence.

We might say that with the will and the dominion of the clairvoyant, as he has had such training in the higher spiritual realms, that he comes into your earth plane with a sufficiency of help from these spiritual realms and that they are ready to stand by and aid him in such research into some particular person's past lives or his Akashic, as it is termed. Now as this individual has evolved into many planes of spiritual consciousness and we are assuming that most of the vortexes within his psychic body are of a sufficiently strong spiritual nature that they have remained somewhat imperishable for several hundred years at least, there is a reasonable chance of success that the clairvoyant can peer into this Akashic and reveal to the person just exactly what his particular trouble is. If he suffers some particular mental aberration or disarrangement which the earth physicians and doctors know little or nothing about and that such corrective therapies are necessary for treatment, then of course it is quite obvious that we must find the cause. Corrective therapy cannot be applied until such causations are accurately determined and a true course of action is determined upon. Some of these processes of action were revealed to you in your previous visit into the scientific sections of the city of Parhelion.

There you actually witnessed the dissection of a thought form body from the psychic body of a young woman. However, all obsessions and various complications which arise from the numerous evolutions into the consciousness of some individual are not necessarily so drastically interwoven with the spurious thought form bodies or even with the lower elemental orders. Usually such separations can be brought about very quickly and very easily with the interjection or proper application of such radiant energy ray beams and things of such nature. Such a low order of astral force will be immediately, shall I say, frightened away or he may tear himself somewhat violently loose from his prey in which case the person is left somewhat discomfited or may be nauseated and sickened. Therefore, reading the Akashic records means simply that we have a complete collaboration with the clair-

336

voyant who is undertaking the particular task of determining such conditions in the Akashic records of the individual.

When the proper forces and motions are brought into play, these libraries which you have visited ofttimes serve a very definite need and fulfillment of purpose in such revelations. It is here, of course, that the individual in question has often placed the records of his life. It is in such cases that we can very easily contact the records of his life and thus very quickly place within the mind of the clairvoyant such pictures as are pertinent to the revelation which is necessary at the time.

I would not have you understand for one moment that such happenings are memory consciousness, either from any person's present earth life or in any previous lives which he may have lived upon your earth plane, and that these happenings just floated loosely around in the atmosphere or the ethers around this person, nor are they attached into his memory consciousness. They are first impingements or wave forms in his psychic body. These, in turn, link him with his true memory consciousness which is his Akashic record as he has written it with his own hand and his own spiritual consciousness in the spiritual realms in which he has made his previous evolutions. I am taking it for granted, of course, that you understand that such a person in question has made a sufficiently large number of self initiations in his upward evolution or flight into the spiritual realms of consciousness, that his psychic body is of a more spiritual nature and that he has as a consequence evolved in some of the spiritual planes as well as in some of the lower orders of material planes.

Now I believe our purpose here in this particular section at this time has been somewhat fully served. I would not go too far because I would not like to bore you with what may be a seemingly repetitious succession of such experiences as might be termed teaching or of such a nature. One striking difference here in this section of course as you have noticed, has been the lack or the absence of such healing therapies as you have witnessed in the other sections or on the planet Venus. There, of course, they were dedicated to spiritual and physical therapies of all kinds. Here we are devoted entirely to the artistic sciences.

Now I believe that we will take our little trip into the lower planet of Muse, where you will see what might be properly called something of the higher astral world of those who have expressed some counterpart, or in some particular way made a number of evolutions in their particular field of endeavor, such as is related to the various five branches of the arts as we have described them here. As this planet is very closely attached, shall I say, with a beam to the entrance or doorway of this section of Parhelion, it is a very easy matter for us to make an immediate appearance upon this planet. However, before we arrive fully at our destination, we will pause somewhere about half way between in what is called distance or space and there we can view rather objectively the panorama which is before us which is rather unusual. As the planet of Muse is different from some of the others which you may witness in your travels, this planet itself or the central part is actually a huge glowing orb of some pinkish-looking crystalline substance. This also, like Eros, seems to pulsate and to expand and contract in some peculiar fashion just as the planet you have just left seems to do.

There is another very unusual sight about this planet and that it has five smaller planets revolving around it, or that they seem to revolve. These planets are something like the moons which revolve around the earth. I shall explain their purpose later as they are the more elemental planes in which the newly evolved souls, from their various earth planes after they have made the emergence from the flesh, come into these smaller satellites which are in the orbit around the larger sun or planet. For lack of a better name, we will call these new arrivals plebeians. They are, of course, such people as have expressed a relative part of their art in the lower earth planes to such a point where they have somewhat dissolved the bonds of their more carnal and materialistic natures, such as have revolved around family organizations and the close attachments of what is sometimes called blood ties. The loosening of these ties makes a person somewhat more free in his spiritual expressions and leaves them in a more jurisdictional attitude whereby they can seem to choose and to discern somewhat better their true course of progression.

So it is with those who have arrived from these lower astral worlds or from the lower material worlds from whence they have lost their physical form or their physical flesh. Thus they will appear first in these smaller moons which are revolving around the large center planet.

Now let us make a landing on the nearest one of these smaller planets or moons. Now that we have our feet more or less planted firmly on the surface, we will begin to see that it is devoted purely to the science and the expression of painting or art. As you will notice when you look about you, there is everything that might inspire a painter such as the one who was called Landseer or to others who liked to paint the various beautiful scenes of nature such as mountains, trees, woods, streams and lakes. This particular little planet is beautiful beyond all description. Even some of the previous sights are somewhat eclipsed by the very soft and wonderful beauty in which you find yourself now.

Over all seems to be somewhat of a roseate or a pinkish haze which gives somewhat like an Indian summer appearance to the landscapes. There are many walks and paths. There are very many high and rugged peaks. There are some which seem to be snow-capped. There are very wonderful and beautiful cloud formations and although the atmosphere would not respond to spectroanalysis, yet there is an atmosphere here in a sense of the word, although it is not one in which you would breathe.

The artist who has emerged into this smaller planet will find himself in such ideal conditions as will truly inspire the innermost reaches of his nature. He will be able to wander about with his palette, his paints and his canvases and paint to the fullest abundance of his nature. If he happens to be such a person who has more or less concentrated his energies and talents into portraits or things of still life which are more of an enclosed or, shall I say, somewhat of a studio nature, he too will find these things because there are small communities and cities scattered about over the face of this small planet which are very natural in their habitat. You might think yourself in Greenwich Village or in some other section of some city which is devoted to the life of the artist. Later on perhaps after a large number of years, if we can use your earth equation of time, the artist plebeian will find himself further inspired to seek newer and more enlarged fields of endeavor. He will therefore find himself after his initiation onto the large planet where he will be ready to participate into such activities as are a little more expansive in nature and thus it will be that he will gradually work and evolve into some of the higher dimensions. He may even eventually find himself in the section of Parhelion from whence we just emerged and there, as you have seen, he may function as a student or as a teacher.

Now we are going to do more or less of a hop, skip, and jump around the four remaining small moons or satellites as we wish to devote some more time to the large central planet which is somewhat of a sun, in a sense of the word. As each one of these other four asteroids or moons are used in their expression of their own relative science, our next jump will be into the one which is devoted to music. Here again you will find that the plebeian or the newly emerged person who has come from some lower earth plane is still fired and imbued with all the enthusiasm of his world of music. Here again we will find certain conditions as are most stimulating to his nature. He will be able to work with his music in such conditions of environment which will be most conducive to the fullest production and inspiration of his nature. Here we may not find the full pastoral beauty which we found on the little planet which was devoted to art and painting but nevertheless, it is almost equally as beautiful. Here again the same beautiful subtle shades of pink, rose and gold seem to flood the atmosphere.

We find small communities and villages and larger places which might be called small cities. Here the musician finds himself in such suitable company where he can continually collaborate and express to the fullest measure and to his greatest heart's delight all of the various things which relate to his musical world. He may find himself in such company as will be productive of orchestrations or he may be producing such things as symphonies or concertos or whatever type of music which best suits him at his particular stage of evolution, so he shall find himself in such environment and thus it will be, until the time comes when he too shall feel the urge and the need to evolve into a more expanded state of consciousness. Then he will find himself in the center planet and so on; the process will be repeated.

So thus it will be with the three remaining small planets which are of literature, sculpturing and drama. In each case, there too we will find the most compatible conditions which will inspire and further induce the plebeian to his greatest and fullest efforts. However, I see that I have gone somewhat beyond the limits of this particular transmission so may I say, rest in the fullest measure of God's love.

A happy day to you, brother and sister. I believe we discontinued our exploration of our particular center of Parhelion somewhere in the vicinity of the sub-planets which were related to the main center or planet of Muse. Taking up where we left off, we have just discovered that these sub-planets were something in the nature of halfway stations, we might call them, between the astral worlds below and to the actual center of Muse. It was there that the initiates who had gone through many evolutions in their various reincarnations had at least arrived to the point where they could emerge into these sub-planetary systems such as they were related into the five various sections of the inspirational arts as we have so classified them in previous discussions. It was here that we also discovered that these sub-planets were of such nature that the initiate or the plebeian could find himself or herself in such conditions which were of the most inspirational nature and more conducive and in harmony with that particular type of spiritual expression in which he or she were so engaged in participating.

It can be said also that these sub-planets were places in which the individual more or less rehabilitated himself or readjusted himself to such a point or position where he could determine whether he would like to proceed onward or whether he would like to reincarnate again into a lower earth plane and to thus work out some of the knowledge which was pertinent to his expression.

These factors all, of course, are determined by the individual himself. He will evolve in his intelligence to such a point where the correlative advice of the teachers who are functioning in these various centers will advise him to or not to reincarnate into the earth planes or to other such sundry positions and such activities of an educational nature shall be entered into which will best befit him. Should he or she determine for themselves that they should reincarnate into an earth plane expression, they would therefore wait and learn and to further adjust themselves to the point in which they would be able to enter into the earth plane through the conception and the doorway of the womb. This, of course, may or may not take what would be called a time period of several hundred years. However, in any case after the emergence in the earth plane, such an individual would be an outstanding exponent of his particular art in whatever field he was actively participating.

Now we have roughly discussed and found out the various functional orders of these sub-planets which are revolving or, rather, I would not use the word revolving, as they do not actually revolve but have, just as in the case of the other more highly evolved planets, such a frequency characteristic which determines their particular position—we shall now go directly to the central planet of Muse and there we shall find out more of how the various relative factors enter into the numerous concepts in which the individual expresses himself in the inspirational arts.

I will not attempt to confuse you by using such terms which are relative to the size or to the position in which the planet occupies in your particular galaxy of star clusters. Let us just say that in the case of Eros that it is very sufficient as to its own size and its function in its relative order or sequence of functions to the various other material planets as well as the astral worlds which are in somewhat of a lower rate of vibration. The planet of Muse occupies, roughly speaking, the same position as Venus in its rate of vibration and it is somewhat, if I can use the term, more materialistic than is in the case of Eros. Here we also find a rather highly developed or a spiritually evolved type of atmosphere and in such formation we shall find also the more familiar cloud structures which are reminiscent of the time you were on Venus. Such is all, however, that there is the general sense of the pervading Radiant Energy which seems to glow and to pulsate and throb into everything about you. The heavens themselves seem to be just a canopy of this pulsating Radiant Energy in which these beautiful varicolored cloud formations seem to float. We have made contact with the planet and descended onto the surface in what might be called a fairly large community or city. As you will see, it is somewhat reminiscent of the more highly developed suburban areas in some of the earth plane expressions, except of course, there are the same outstanding differences as to the nature of materials which enter into the various dwellings and buildings which you see about you. Here they are, as on Venus, constructed of the same beautifully crystalline substance with which you have now become familiar, all in a variety or a kaleidoscope of color which defies description.

The streets themselves or thoroughfares are well laid out. There are none of the familiar gutters which you might associate with collecting refuse or debris, as there is none such of these substances to be found in these planets. Like in all of the more highly evolved planets, the intelligent Radiant Energies themselves are of such nature that there is no precipitation of dust or other such debris as you might find on the material planets. Looking about on the street you will see various personages, both male and female, children and adults who seem to be conducting their lives in more or less of a leisurely fashion just as they might be doing in some of your more familiar earth planets. You may be a little surprised at this and yet they are all, of themselves, rather highly evolved souls or personages, all of whom have at least become first or second Initiates.

You will find as we progress farther into the central part of this city that there are various types of large halls, theaters and outdoor amphitheaters or coliseum-like structures which are devoted to the expressions of the different arts which you may find in this city. There are no sectional differences in these cities and there are many and numerous of them which are scattered about in various places of more or less advantageous situations throughout the surface of this planet. When I say there are no sectional differences, I mean that you are quite likely to wander into one home, you may find someone very studiously studying his particular musical instrument, whatever the case may be, and in going into the neighbor's home which is some distance away you may find that here is an artist who is creating some masterpiece on the canvas. In any case, however, there is a complete unison and a complete integration of these various associated arts. There are none of the frictions which you might think might be found in some of the lower or more materialistic earth plane orders.

The people here, as I have said, have long since left the position in their lives when such elements of jealousy or other such things which pertain to the earth-life existence have long since been eliminated from their consciousness, nor do the various inhabitants of these communities express anything in the nature of the lower order of sex as it has been expressed in your earth plane. The order of sex here is, as it has been previously explained, conducted in the biocentric fashion. Many of the artists or playwrights, dramatists and various other differences in the associated inspirational arts often find their biocentric counterpart in these cities and thus they live together very harmoniously and find a complete unison in their art. There are also many and numerous activities which are connected with the expression of these arts in a large and rather a public way.

To live in one of these communities for any length of time, you would find a complete succession of participations in such stage presentations or in such exhibits in art galleries and things of such a functional nature. There are also a great number of festivals and artistic carnivals of different kinds, all of which are carried on and conducted in a very high order of expression. They might remind you sometimes and be somewhat reminiscent of some of the pageants or festivals which you may have seen on your earth plane. But here again, the difference is that they are very highly evolved and very spiritual in nature by comparison and that you will, in consequence, have to somewhat change your line of thought in the participation and viewing of such festivals, carnivals, pageants and other activities. In other words, it is here that the people, as they are Initiates, carry out to the fullest degree their particular expression in the inspirational arts. There are also other factors which are vitally pertinent and which are interconnected and interwoven with such expressions. It is not all play and no work, as we might say, as there is a great deal of the more constructive work which expands the individual consciousness of each individual into the higher dimensions and realms of his particular expression. It is here also that many of the teachers and students from the center of Parhelion which we have just visited often come to renew or to again express to the lower orders of these people you find in the cities somewhat of the knowledge and wisdom which they have gained in the centers above them.

It will be also that many of the people who have thus emerged into these various cities in the planet of Muse will in time evolve in their consciousness until they can also assume the position of a teacher and thus they will emerge into the higher center of Parhelion thus to conduct their own expression or activity in a teacher's relationship. As this particular transmission was intended merely as a continuance of the previous one in which we had to terminate for lack of time, I will merely say that such information which we have already gained should be slowly assimilated, so therefore let us discontinue for the present while we again arrange things into such consequence and order where a new visitation and exploration can be so participated in. So until such further time, rest with the fullest measure of God's Love.

CHAPTER 45

Greetings, dear friends, this is Robert. You know, Elizabeth just wasn't happy until I took over something of a transmission or became the guide for one of our tours. However, I would warn you that it might be a short one. We are very thrilled that we have the opportunity of speaking to you people on the earth. It was just about a hundred years ago that we were there on the jolly old earth, but before we get into this tour, I have a little secret that I would like to divulge and I don't think the person involved would mind at all. She is a very shy person and that is probably the reason why she did not reveal her true identity. I am speaking of Iona. I believe she conducted a couple of your tours. She is, as she said, the biocentric of Hilarion. Her real identity is Eliason. She actually works in another position in Parhelion somewhere around on the other side, the number two gate, I believe, and has something to do with the education of children. However, she does come in occasionally on demand or whenever circumstances are such that there is a particular need for her services. Elizabeth and I were a bit chagrined after our last tour to find that we had completely forgotten to take you into the museums or libraries of the two centers we have visited, so with your kind indulgence, we will start where we began in the section which is devoted to literature. We were somewhat overwhelmed by the ceremony of initiation of the group of people who became neophytes to live among us.

Now the section here as we have reentered which is devoted to literature and embodies those arts which are relative to something which has to do with writing, such as poetry, prose and the various different types of writings which are fiction and nonfiction as this was explained to you somewhat as we walked along by Elizabeth.

Now let us go up into a floor which is above these many classrooms and see something of the museum. We have determined to make you very thoroughly acquainted with our beautiful city while you are here because these opportunities just don't come along every day. Naturally we are very proud and take a good deal of civic interest in what goes on about us. This pride is of course justifiable. As we progress you will see that we have a great deal about which to be proud. Now we are up in the library or the museum above the main floor where we will see what progress man has made in his various facets and phases of his literary efforts through the ages. Like in many of the great museums and libraries you have already visited, the vastness and size seems to overwhelm you and it is the same here as it is in many other places. Now here is a corridor where you see there are a lot of glass cases, something similar to those you saw in Parhelion. Here we will see the first birch bark writings of some of the more primitive forms of man as he wrote his various word pictures with a piece of charcoal on some piece of bark or a very convenient stone. Here are clay tablets which came from the pre-Babylonian era. This little clay tablet, just in case you are interested, happens to be a love letter from some swain who was courting some fair young maid. You can imagine what a young lady of your time would think if she received such a letter because it weighs about five pounds. Going on a bit further we see various types of writing. Here is an example of Sanskrit. It is a very ancient language and had its origin from some of the other planets in the solar system. We see examples of the early Egyptian hieroglyphs or the glyphic forms of writing. We also see types of Aramaic and ancient Chinese and such various and sundry examples of the more primitive types of writing, if we can call them such, which have existed on your earth plane. You will notice, however, that there is a striking resemblance in some forms of writings. For instance, the figure of this eagle on the totem pole of the Alaskan Indian is the same as the Thunderbird of the Zuni and is also depicted as a sacred bird in the Aztec religion. You will find it also emblazoned on the shields and on the chariots of the ancient Egyptians.

Now, of course, all these languages and writings had their origin in the ancient root races of the world and of other worlds and planetary systems. But let us go on a little further into the archives of this vast library which you see before you. They are all books which are dealing relatively with not only your earth plane but with a number of other planets which are revolving in different solar systems. They are a little different than the books you saw in the library in Parhelion inasmuch as these are more reasonable facsimiles of the original books. The leaves, as you turn this volume here, seem to be more like the original paper-like substance with which you are familiar in your earth plane books, also the size is more relative to such books. And so as we look up and down these great corridors, we see numbers of students and Initiates who are browsing among these books and great shelves of this huge and immense library. They are all learning something of the drama, the art, the poetry and the various other facets of the literary science which deals with the histories of many races and evolutions of mankind in many planetary systems.

Now that we have obtained somewhat of a more prospective view of this center, let us go next door to the one which was somewhat visited in our previous exploration, the one which is devoted to the various inspirational sciences which can be classed roughly as drama. Drama in a true sense means stage presentations, plays, pageantry or various other types of exhibitions which denote some message or form from some facet of human life such as it exists in the immediate environment to which it is associated. On your earth through the Renaissance of a hundred or so years ago, there was a great upheaval not only in the literary world but in the musical world as well, so thus we find there were great stage presentations of many operas.

There were great revivals of folk music and dancing. There were also enlarged endeavors in the field of ballet and other forms of Terpsichore. Let us peer in one of these rooms we are passing by because I would like you to see who is teaching and who is interested in directing the choreography of this particular ballet. As you see the figures on the stage as we enter this room are depicting your familiar Swan Lake Ballet. The master himself is Tschaikovsky. He, of course, belongs next door in the section which is devoted to music but he often comes over here and conducts a class when it is something of special interest to him, such as the one we are seeing now as it was originally written and composed by him on your earth plane, and so he is naturally in the best position to so conduct the choreography and explain the libretto of this wonderful and beautiful ballet.

The participants themselves, are, of course, the people who are something more than the neophytes. They are learning the more intricate and inward expressions of these ballets in a spiritual sense so that they will be able to more fully enter in and capture the true meaning and spiritual values such as they were interwoven by the composer at the time of their conception.

The floor above these many classrooms and stages is also devoted to, shall I say, the museum. I don't like the word museum but we have to use it here as it is the nearest thing which we can get to describing a place where we store such things which are relative to this expression. In getting up to this level, we see just as we might expect that all of the things here are more or less done in miniature. You saw some of these things in the city of Parhelion—small cases, where there were electronically activated figurines or mannequins which went through the various acts and stage presentations. Here there are numerous of these scenes also but a great deal of space is also devoted to the full-life presentations of these various types of the dramatic forms and the inceptions of such eras of expression, if they can be termed such.

William Shakespeare, as you know, ushered in a whole new age in the field of dramatic art in his various plays and was rather closely followed in several other different authorships as they appeared in your earth plane in later periods of time. Shakespeare, of course, is immortal because he truly portrayed the more fundamental concepts of man's nature. These are just the same today as they were in his time, however, I see that you are just a little impatient to visit the section which is devoted to music which is just next door and so I will leave the readers to more or less fill in the various other things which can be seen about this large hallway which is devoted to portraying the spiritual science of drama. My only regret in this circumstance of our exploration is that we cannot devote more time to a fuller and more complete exploration of these various centers. The whole city itself and the life here as we live it would be very worthy of a large volume all by itself; however, the book in its entirety, as I have been so informed, will be one of a very large size and indeed it must be so, because it embraces the seven different functions of the Shamballa which have long been a mystery to the people of the earth. It is, as you have begun to find out, a huge and vast project to portray even the smallest fraction of the various functions and the many facets which are relative to these different centers.

Now we have finally arrived into the great hall of the huge section which is devoted to the expression of various types and forms of music. Don't expect to see jive or be-bop here. This type of music is strictly, as Elizabeth said, a degenerative form which is born out of some psychological principles of rebellion in the minds of the younger generation on the earth plane. However, we are dealing with many different types of music here which are of the more inspirational nature. We shall find out something of the nature of the operas and of the ballets and while they may seem to be very closely related to the field of dramatic art, indeed they are so, for one would be useless without the other. Could we imagine an opera being portrayed without music or could we imagine it being portrayed without drama? Nor would a ballet function any differently or fare any better and so it is that these two spiritual sciences are very closely interwoven.

It is at this particular point I would like to point out that many of the more advanced students in music who have come from your earth and other earths finally make their appearance here and study in their many and various related facets in such musical fields of endeavor in which they have embarked. You will find many of your foremost orchestra leaders, composers and other expressionists who are studying and who are actually reenacting something, in a higher and more evolved spiritual state of consciousness, of the life which they portrayed in your musical world on the earth. Here we see the great masters such as Beethoven, Brahms, Bach and others who make appearances and teach classes at regular intervals.

We have some of the others who are somewhat of the lesser or lower initiates who also conduct regular forums or classes and exhibitions. We find men from your earth plane and women, such as Paganini, Clara Schumann and her dearly espoused husband. Tschaikowsky makes his appearance at very regular and frequent intervals. I could name a whole host of other musical composers who have at different times appeared in your earth plane and left behind them vast treasures and wealth of music. You might say Mendelssohn, Handel and others who are quite well-known, although they are in somewhat of an advanced mastership, yet they too make their appearance and conduct regular class work.

As we wander about these various great corridors and halls which have been roughly called classrooms, we see actual orchestras in full function led by some rather prominent leaders, several of whom I have just mentioned. We also find that there is a great deal of individual instruction and in some cases, the instructors become the pupils when the higher Masters come in from Parhelion or from other higher dimensions, which they do occasionally, and teach some of the higher forms of the musical art. To you musical expressionists on the earth plane and who are so vitally interested in this inspirational science, may I say to you that there is a whole new age of understanding in this realm which is just coming into the consciousness of the earth plane people. Scientifically speaking, we call this the field of vibrotherapy or the healing art such as it is induced by outward stimulation from musical sources. These principles are somewhat known to some of the earth people at this time, however, they have just only partially begun to explore this vast new field of vibrotherapy.

In the coming generations and for hundreds of years you will find entirely new forms of music which will be springing up and which will deal much more directly with such fields as are relative with nature and with the higher spiritual realms of creation. It has been a long time since there has been any really worthwhile music produced on your earth plane as compared with the masters who flourished a hundred or two years ago but you may rest assured your day is coming in the future. There are great numbers of students and teachers in this center who will, in the course of the next few hundred years, reincarnate into your earth plane and teach a whole new vital concept of music, one which will exceed your fondest dreams. It is also almost needless to add that there will be a great number of new types of musical instruments which will also come into use and expression. These musical instruments will be more of the electronic nature and will be manipulated or controlled in their expressions by the musicians who have learned the subtle form and art of controlling these musical instruments to their utmost capacity.

Elizabeth and I, as you know, devote most of our efforts in the field of poetry. We have been quite successful in some small way in doing a bit of teaching to some of the younger students. Our city of Coralanthea is unique in some ways. You will find great numbers of children here and particularly at this time as it is quite obvious that your earth plane today is going through its evolution toward a new high spiritual goal and must needs have a new race or a new type of people to live in such a world. The students that we have here are of the younger generation which will form the future generations of your new world.

Now that you have obtained somewhat of an idea of this section which is devoted to music, let us go next door to the section which is devoted to art. You will wonder why art was not included with sculpturing as they are both rather closely related in many respects. Well, we can say in a broad sense of the word that all of these inspirational sciences are very closely related but it serves a good purpose if we separate them in their true perspective as it gives each individual student a much better chance to completely channel his own talent. In the section which is devoted to art, as you would naturally expect, here we find art as it is expressed to its fullest measure. With the exception of Parhelion, I doubt whether you will find any place in the immediate universe, if I can use this word at this time, which would so adequately express in the relationship of your earth plane understanding what is meant by the true concepts of art. Just as in the other centers, we find many of the old masters of your earth plane. They have been named somewhat to some degree; if you will consult your encyclopedia or history books, you could probably add a hundred or more names to those already named. They are either functioning here, living here, studying or teaching, just as in the case of the other inspirational arts.

So let us step into this nearest doorway into the (pardon the term) classroom where we will see something going on which will express how it is that art is taught or studied here in this section. This is like some of the other places you have visited, more like a large vast gallery rather than a room. Here you will see wonderful and beautiful pastoral scenery which is very inspirational in nature, just as in many of the other places where these inspirational sciences are taught. We have devoted much thought and time to suitably constructing these rooms so they will be most conducive and inspirational to the students and teachers. Going about, we find individually and collectively in groups various neophytes or students and their teachers or we may find a single artist with his easel and brushes and palette very busily engaged in portraying some facet of life as he sees it upon his canvas. Going into some of the other rooms we shall also find students who are studying the various chemistries which go into the making and mixing of paints, pigments and colors.

Such things are very necessary and vital if an artist is to portray the real esoterical values on his canvas. Art is not wholly confined to the portrayal or expression of paints or water colors upon canvas or paper but art also expresses itself in hundreds of other different ways. We may find artists here who are delicately tracing a beautiful design in some object of ceramic art. We may also find such things as are more closely related to the section which is devoted to sculpturing. As students here will also begin to learn the various different designs both ancient and modern which have gone into the art of silver and goldsmithing. We may also find out it is that an artist first learns how to carve the head of a Mona Lisa on a cameo and so it is that many students, while they are not strictly confined to this section, very often pass back and forth from this section to the one which is next door, which is devoted to the art of sculpturing.

I had hoped to finish this transmission by including the last of these sections. However, I see that you are beginning to tire somewhat so, for the present moment, with God's great love, rest in peace.

CHAPTER 46

Cheerio to you, brother and sister. This is Robert again. Elizabeth scolded me a little for keeping you so long last night on our previous tour but she also added that as I had done such a good job, I must take over again for the conclusion of our visit here to Coralanthea. Now let's see, I believe we were somewhere in the artistic section when we discontinued, so what do you say if we get on with it and go right to the center which is devoted to sculpturing. I was a bit surprised, just as you will be, when you see what sculpturing really is. A long time ago I thought that sculpturing was just some man hammering on a piece of rock with a chisel and mallet but that is not the case. Now that we are entering into this large section, as you see it is like the others, constructed of that very beautiful pink or coral-colored crystal. The building itself is like the others of a huge or an immense size. Now, getting into the doorway proper, we are standing in the main and central corridor. On each side of this corridor are the many, numerous and different classrooms. Let us duck into this nearest one here and see just what is going on. I have been here before so I am not entirely unaware. However, you may be somewhat amazed. This classroom, as you see, is also of a very huge and immense size. Here there are various students and instructors who are learning the art of the lapidary or the carving or sculpturing and facing of the various semi-precious stones which are found not only on your earth plane but on the many earth planes with which we are associated. It may be of interest to you to note that there is a wonderful bit of science attached to the carving and facing of all of these precious gems that, in themselves, are crystals and assume various geometrical forms and shapes. The lapidary has to learn the lines of cleavage and how to properly so face the stones as to bring out their inward radiance and beauty. He is also made acquainted with such factors as the coloration of the stones, as these colors are the result of various chemical combinations of other elements which enter in at the time of the infusion or the inception of these crystal structures in the volcanic or cataclysmic eruptions on the earth plane.

Such things as iron, aluminum, gold and other elements which enter in give these gems their brilliant coloration. About the hardest thing on your earth is a diamond and about the only thing that will cut a diamond is another diamond. Here is a student who is busily engaged on a wheel-like contrivance where he is using diamond dust to face a diamond. He is learning the processes which will later enable him to reincarnate into the earth plane and thus display a great deal of this science and talent. Now let us go into another of these numerous classrooms with which we are associated. Going into this place we will find students and instructors who are engaged in various arts which relate to carving in the different materials as they are found in the various planets. Here is a student who is carving on a bit of ivory. Another student here is shaping something with bone and there are various other innumerable types of carving in the various materials as they are found in the different planets. The many kinds of softer stone such as soapstone are also sometimes carved into numerous shapes which are both ornamental or utilitarian.

Before we proceed any further, however, I would like to philosophize a bit upon your particular earth planet. If I do this, perhaps you may be able to understand just a little more fully what sculpturing is. In studying the histories of your earth planet you will find that many different times in the past, various periods of sculpturing came into expression, a sort of renaissance, as it were. In China there was one period which happened about 6000 years B.C.; in India there was also a great renaissance that came in before the time of Buddha. Many of the Indian temples that you see nowadays, just as the Chinese art which is dedicated to a very flamboyant expression of art which is depicted in the various types of ceramics or vases as cloisonné, so in India they too have gone into great lengths to express their own type of sculpturing and art. The lavish displays of the temples in which you will see a great deal of the mosaic type of sculpturing which means that tiny bits of shells and pearls were so cleverly interlaid as to form beautiful designs or depict certain historical scenes. The exteriors of these temples are carved with an innumerable variety of gargoyles and various symbolic figures, not to mention the spires, minarets and the vast array of very intricate symbolism which enters into the expression of these temples.

Going into Egypt, this may too be somewhat familiar as you have seen pictures of the great stone pyramids, the carvings in the mountains of the various Pharaohs, such as the Ramses. We know of Cleopatra's needle which is an obelisk which is now in the museum in New York. Coming up into your more modern times, just before the time of Christ there was a Grecian renaissance of sculpturing in which the marbles and other types of materials were carved into the innumerable figures of the gods and goddesses who were supposed to be ruling the world at that time. A little later on, there was also an Italian renaissance of such carvings. Your museums today are full of these various marble figures such as the Venus de Milo and others who are more or less familiar historical figures in your history books.

Now here is another section. As we have somewhat discussed the sculpturing in marbles and in stone, we will go into this section and see that there is also another facet which can be said to be very similar to the carving of stone and that is carving of stone in its pure sense. It relates to stone as it enters in as a building material in the many and different edifices upon your earth plane. Here in the ancient times, stone was carved roughly from the mountain quarries in such rectangular or cubistic shape as would best suit the purpose for the building which it was designed to construct. In your more modern recent times, substances of a biolithic nature such as concrete were compounded. The ancient Romans knew of a concrete substance, also they knew of a tar-like composition in Arabia which is something like the asphalt of your streets today. These biolithic compounds are, as the term denotes, compounded of two or more substances, the adhesive and the foundation. In concrete it is the Portland cement with the sand and gravel, so these biolithic compounds are playing a very large and important part in the sculpturing of your modern cities today. Your skyscrapers are frameworks of steel upon which these biolithic compounds are formed to add strength and rigidity.

Now here is another section which is devoted to an expression of sculpturing which is somewhat familiar. This relates to the carving and fashioning of wood and such kindred substances on your earth plane. In a sense of the word, this classroom looks almost like a furniture factory. Here you will see students who are undergoing scholastic teaching which will enable them later to reincarnate into suitable planes of consciousness and thus express their craft as designers in the more utilitarian or functional articles in the home such as the chairs, the davenports and other familiar objects which you see about you. Such instructors here who are teaching have been responsible at a different time in your earth plane of periods of furniture design. I might name two of these as Chippendale and Hepplewhite. Wood also is used in various other phases of sculpturing. The Alaskan Indian constructed his totem pole and his dugout canoe. This was sculpturing. So did the Chinaman who carved the very intricate designs which festooned the ridges on the roofs of his temples, such as was done in teakwood and in other woods of the harder and more compact nature. There are statues and figures existing today which have been constructed thousands of years ago of the harder and more compact woods such as ironwood, that have existed in the temples and shrines of worship for the many centuries. Here we may also see students who are carving beautiful cameos. A cameo, as you know, is the shell of a mollusk which is taken from the bottom of the Mediterranean. The outer shell is stripped off, leaving the coralline substance underneath exposed. The craftsman then proceeds to carve the face of some beautiful woman or some such similar configuration upon the surface of this shell.

Now here is another classroom which we shall enter into. As we have more or less gone rather swiftly for the obvious reasons of time and space which are limited to the length of our transmission or tours. This classroom is devoted to the fashioning of the various types of metals—metallurgy, in other words. Here we see craftsmen or students of all races and from all physical planes who are learning to fashion the various precious and semi-precious metals which are indigenous to that particular planet—such things as gold, silver, lead, platinum and so on. They are learning to draw these materials out into the various shapes which are either ornamental or utilitarian or combine the virtues of both into such things as vases, vessels of various types and shapes, ornamentations for the body such as rings, bracelets, etc. A great deal of art and craftsmanship is necessarily entered into as the designs and shapes of these various types of craftsmanship often enter into very intricate and an amazing array of configurations.

One of the teachers here who is teaching in the classroom which we have just visited, and I would like to interject this little story here at this time because it is very apropos; this particular instructor is of Italian origin from your earth plane and was known as Antoine Canova, if you will pardon the hesitancy there for just a moment. This story relates to the time when this very famous sculptor as a lad was serving an apprenticeship in a tavern in Italy when a nobleman in passing through was very much impressed by the figure of a crouching lion which this youngster had carved in a large chunk of butter and set upon the table before him. So young Antoine was given the advantage of being a protégé to this wealthy nobleman and was thus enabled to bring into the world many and great works of art in the field of sculpturing.

Now if I may indulge your kind patience for just a moment, I will enter into somewhat of a resumé of just what we have previously explored in these five centers of Coralanthea. As it was quite obvious that we could not thoroughly and completely obtain a full view of the many and varied activities going on, I would just like to roughly run over these five centers a little more, as it were, and point out some of the things which were previously somewhat omitted. We are sorry friends, Robert lost control at the beginning of this transmission and it has been carried on by someone else, however, we will explain these things a little more fully later on. And as the power has somewhat been disrupted, let us rest, while we reorganize for a future transmission.

CHAPTER 47

Greetings again, this is the Brownings. Elizabeth is here with me this time. We had some small crisis arise in our previous tour and I was forced to suddenly leave. As you know, Elizabeth and I are teaching a group of students from the earth plane in their astral moments of sleep. It happened that one of the students enjoyed being here so much he was reluctant to leave and so I had to assist Elizabeth in persuading him to return home. However, there was small loss as my very good friend, Robert Louis Stevenson, stepped in. So you see, it was all Robert anyway, wasn't it? Now I think we were about to the point where we were to take up in sort of a summation and to further enlarge or to bring out some very pertinent points which may have been neglected in our previous tours. I have been checking over the lists with Elizabeth and there are a few things.

The first plane we explored, the literary section, was somewhat covered and it is not complicated. We will merely say that the chronology of the worlds, as it is portrayed in the written word of the book form in its numerous facets and phases, would involve a very vital and important subject in itself. But this was somewhat rather thoroughly covered, so let us skip over to the next section which I believe was drama. Here too we explored some of the many facets which are relative to the portrayal of pageantry and plays and things of that nature, however, one important facet was neglected as we did not attach too much importance to it at the time. This is the science and art of motion picture, television and radio as it is portrayed on your earth plane at the present time.

Now I am not one to pass judgment nor will I render any form of condemnation. It is unfortunate that such a wonderful science as it is expressed in the technical phases as well as in the dramatic relationships on your earth is used for the portrayal of the baser and more carnal natures of man. I will not say or make comparisons with Gary Cooper or Humphrey Bogart with such personages as John Wilkes Booth, nor will I say that Lana Turner or Marilyn Monroe could compare with Sarah Bernhardt. The movies of your present age are tailored somewhat to fit the needs of the times. It is, in reality, a psychological equation, as you know the various inhibitions, frustrations and fears, such as they are in the races of mankind on your earth plane are repressed emotional factors and that in attending the movie theaters, they see portrayed on the screen such things as are relative to their own repressed inhibitions. By seeing others perform and do the various things which they are afraid to do or have been repressed in so doing, they feel some sort of a relief or they are somewhat pacified. However, I would say that the outlet of the theater or the motion picture screen, the television and radio could be very wonderful and valuable assets in promulgating and promoting educational and inspirational works of such nature that it would soon change the course of destiny of the races of mankind on your earth plane.

To those who think that such things are relative to your time and place, I would like to say that motion pictures, television and such kindred sciences have been known and are known on other planets in your solar system. Mars has been using television for many thousands of years. There are other planets which have long ago even ceased to exist which, at one time in their destiny or their evolution, used such electronic devices. These planets flourished in the height of their time even millions of years before your own earth planet even knew the first constructive form of life. Do not flatter yourselves, my friends of the earth because you think you have brought into realization some invention or some contrivance. These things always have existed in more or less relative concepts and phases in other dimensions or in other worlds long before there was a realization of time or place as it concerns your earth plane. Now, however, I must not spend too much time in philosophizing. I am going to leave that for a little later on to some of my more worthy colleagues in another planet.

So let us skip on in to the next center which I believe is devoted to music. Here also we explored somewhat the various rooms or dimensions in which the numerous facets of your musical world was expressed. There were also numerous other expressions which related to other worlds or other dimensions with which you were not so familiar. Here was also explained to you some of the principles of vibrotherapy or the healing and stimulating and inspiring nature of sound or music. The secondary wave forms of healing energy which could be superimposed or interwoven with such harmonious conclusions of chords and structures of musical intonations were too vast and innumerable to enter into. This, like many other of the facets of science which relate to the five inspirational arts, would in themselves make up a whole large complete volume and would take many years to do to the fullest conclusion.

Our next section, I believe, was devoted to the

exploration of the more artistic concepts of the earth man and of the other planets in the various solar systems. Now, we do not confuse the term art with a man standing by an easel and daubing paint on a canvas. Here we found out that art expressed itself in an innumerable number of ways. Some of these ways were, of course, not mentioned for the obvious lack of time and space, yet art does express itself in countless thousands of ways in your earth plane. Even the housewife who is interested in harmoniously expressing a decorative scheme of some sort in her house is an artist in her own sense. She is even artistic when she bakes a cake and does so with a great deal of flourish and self-justifiable pride if the cake turns out well.

There is art in every craft and in every expression of life on your earth plane. Even the bricklayer takes a great deal of pride in seeing the completed wall or structure and that the bricks are symmetrically lined up in a complete structural alignment which is very pleasing to his artistic and his scientific eye. We can also say that even the little girl playing with mud pies is expressing a good deal of her artistic temperament and learning the relative values of such factors as placement, background, etc., as she begins her first embryonic expression in your earth plane relationships. Now our last phase, I believe, here relates to sculpturing. Here you found out and explored the different relationships and the different types of sculpturing. However, there was one facet here, I believe, which was not fully entered into.

In your age and your present time, the evolution of the world can be called a synthetic age. There is so much about you in your present age which is either processed or synthetic. You cannot enter any one of your stores which relates to the selling of merchandise of any kind which you find in your homes or which you use in your daily life which has not been processed or is not of a synthetic nature. You ladies wear synthetic clothing, you adorn your faces with synthetic products of the cosmetic nature and thus if I can say, you are also artisans or artists in your own sense of the word. Your homes are decorated with many of the synthetic products which are of a very artistic nature. In your kitchens you find many synthetic or plastic materials which have entered into your daily lives in the past few years. All these products and their understanding and usage is, in a sense, a relationship of art and sculpturing. Such utilitarian forms and decorative forms of these synthetic and plastic-like materials have also existed in other earth worlds or in other such material dimensions long before the time of your earth. The old saying that there is nothing new under the sun is very factually true. Those of you who are living in the earth plane today, are in a large way, merely repeating the evolution and course of such similar worlds which have existed in other solar systems in the countless ages of time which have long since passed.

And so for such future explorations of the other centers of our Shamballa, if we here in Coralanthea have omitted any of the factors which you seem to feel were necessary or which would need further explanation, I believe you have no need to fear. Such explanations in the future transmissions will be given to you. I believe also that as you read these lines and such concepts and factors are entered into that you will be able, in a large sense, to fill in some of the vacant places, as it is obviously impossible in one narration or in one book to give you a complete and factual word picture of all that takes place in these seven centers of Shamballa. So until such future time, may I say that it has indeed been a great pleasure that we have renewed our contact and our friendship and our feeling of brotherly love with you earth plane people in your new world and in your new time.

When we were on your earth, things were not as they are now. We did not have the electrical conveniences or the automobiles that you people have now. Our life was comparatively simple. We lived by candlelight or by lamplight. We centered our life around the open fireplace. Home was a place which was conducive and harmonious to the fullest and most pleasant experiences of our lives. We almost feel a sense of pity for you people who have so complicated and confounded your lives with the thouands of your civilized appurtenances. Such things have been, as we could say, a two-edged sword, one that has seemed at the time to be a convenience and yet has in the end only served to lop off a portion of your peace of mind. We believe that in the future that much of these things which you consider necessities or even luxuries will pass off into the oblivion of history and that the more spiritual values of life will return to you earth people. And with the passing of this mechanical and electronic age and all of the monsters which you have created for yourself, you will find the return of the dove of Peace not only among your nations but within your own selves and in the relationship of your heart and your mind with the great spiritual and inspirational force which you call God. So until such time, we the Brownings and all here in Coralanthea bid you, not adieu, but until we see you again, in God's greatest love, may you live in Peace.

CHAPTER 48

Auka Makaula to you, brothers and sisters. Just in case my greeting startled you, it is merely a salutation which means, the Peace of God be with you. It is a little greeting which is customarily used in the ancient languages which existed on your earth plane thousands of years ago in the ancient lands of India and Tibet. My identity is Maha Chohan, as I was known in the histories of the earth plane of a long-ago age of India. We welcome you to the third section of Shamballa and the symbol above the entrance way which you see as you are about to enter is the torch which is held by the hand giving light to the world. Please enter in and feel that you are most heartily welcome, for indeed it is so. We have long awaited this opportunity but come sit here beside this fountain of radiant energies. While your eyes become accustomed, I will explain to you something more of the mysteries of heaven and earth just as they have been promised that they would be given to you. There have been many questions which have been occurring and recurring in your minds which are associated with the mysteries of the Eastern world. To you Western minds, it is indeed a paradox that those who call themselves Christians and read in the Bible that they know so little of the inner mysteries of life and of these things which have been written and practiced for many hundreds of thousands of years on your earth, long before your Bible was instituted.

I will attempt to clear up some of the mysteries which are attached to the Eastern theologies as they are expressed in such concepts of Buddhism or Brahmanism as you know them in the Western language. You were rightly led into somewhat of the more theosophical explanations as they exist in your earth books and in the tenets of the minds which so deciphered and were conceived in them through inspiration. But it is my purpose to further simplify such knowledge and wisdom as it is far too vast and too preponderant in its expression and terminology to mean little or nothing to the average Western mind. As you have been told, our purpose is to simplify and to completely denude any mysticism or esoterically evolved concepts which may have arisen to confound the many earth minds who have, as a consequence, been at a loss to properly orient their minds into some semblance of a spiritual philosophy which would give them greater advantage over the problems of the various reincarnations.

To you who are on the path of truth, may I salute you and may I wish you and project to you all the intensities and the strength of the love of the Immortal God. As I have detected in your minds that you have wondered much as to the progress of the cycles of reincarnations and to the names which have been attached to the various Avatars or exponents of spiritual philosophy in your earth plane and so, for your benefit and others, I will clear up some of these mysteries for you.

I may begin with Osiris who existed as the Sun God or 'Ra' in the Egyptian spiritual concepts ten or twelve thousand years ago or even beyond that time. The story is one which follows a strange parallel to many of the Avatars who have appeared on the earth plane and that they have all been born into and conceived of such immaculate or 'divine' conception. So it was in the time of the worship and spiritual theology as it was expressed in Egypt at that time. Osiris overshadowed Isis who was mother of earth so that she bore the son Horus. It was Horus who later reincarnated into the land of Egypt as Hermes and for which we have named this particular section of the Shamballa and called it Hermes as it relates to the great philosophical and spiritual interpretations which were collected together. Hermes, in a word, conforms much with Kung Fu or Confucius in the collection of the philosophical works which relate to the spiritual interpretations of mankind in Egypt at his time. Please do not confound him with the Hermes of the Grecian era, who came later.

If you will count on your fingers, I can name off those who have appeared on your earth plane as Avatars or Messiahs. You have confounded also the term or the phrase Buddha which, in itself, means a spiritual leader or a Messiah in its pure sense. There have been seven Buddhas who have reincarnated on your earth at different times. Such as they are, they have become the spiritual leaders and directors of the Shamballa, and while we here in expressing these as the seven personal identities are doing so under the direct control and cooperation with the inner conclave of the thirty-three Logi, who are ruling several thousand other planets besides your own earth plane in a natural sequence and evolution of cycles which revolve into countless and innumerable numbers of reincarnations from earth plane to earth plane among the races of mankind. Some such theory was expounded by one of our colleagues here who is, in this plane at this moment, a Grecian philosopher by the name of Plato. Plato, as you know, was a student of Socrates who is also teaching in this center at this time. So it was with these various seven, one who is known as Zoroaster, who became Lord Maitreya and rules the seventh plane. This is not known to your earth people at this time. It was Krishna who later became known as Hilarion. The Gautama Buddha, who you know as the man who sat under the fig tree six hundred years before the Avatar Christ, later reincarnated as an immaculate conception and was known as the Shankara and who also lived the same number of years as the Avatar Jesus, thirty-two years.

The great Manu, himself, has his identity buried in the unwritten pages of history, which concerns a civilization which is directly linked to the Oriental version of Shamballa which existed in a great civilization half a million years ago in the northern reaches of Tibet or Southern Mongolia. It is said that this city was destroyed but it was not so. It was carried into heaven. The elements of the buildings and all of the people were transmuted into higher elemental substances and so it became one of the teaching esoterical planes which is part of one of the present Shamballas. Manu is further personified in the books of the ancient Indian teachings as they are revealed in the writings which relate to the various translations and works of the Veda. You will read of them in other works on your earth plane but to avoid confusion I will avoid going into them too deeply as I know this work is appealing to a great mass of people who are, for a large part, only earnestly seeking the first step of becoming an initiate. (Please rest now for a moment but do not terminate this transcription as I will return shortly.)

We will continue. A few moments ago I was explaining to you some of the mysteries of reincarnation as it regarded or affected those who were working in the higher realms and dimensions and who were known to you by such titles as Lords or Masters. I also mentioned factors which related to the reincarnations from such material and physical worlds with which we worked at one particular time so that through each incarnation as we gained strength and wisdom, it was necessary, and through the call of mankind through the epochs of time on these earth planes, that we must come again and again in physical form. The reasons for these appearances are sometimes very obvious as you will study the New Testament of your Bible and see that at that time the appearance of the Avatar Christ was of the utmost importance. I might say also that these reincarnations or appearances into the lower material planes serve a twofold purpose, inasmuch as they too help us to solidify and to further consolidate such concepts and wisdom as we have succeeded in learning in the higher spiritual realms.

In the second section of Parhelion, it is at the present time supervised by the person who you called on your earth plane, Buddha. Before, however, you get to that particular section of Parhelion, I would like you to know that a much better name for him would, of course, be Shankara such as he is known here among us. Now enough of this for the present. A little later on we will go through the various centers or as they have been called classrooms here in this section which relates to the philosophical philosophies or doctrines of the many earth planes and we shall meet some of the, shall I say, ancient Grecian or pre-Grecian philosophers as well as some of the more modern or contemporary exponents who have contributed somewhat to a more factual and better way of life.

We will continue these tours on the premise and the understanding that we come to you not as personages who would deliver to the earth plane any sundry or new expressions of such philosophies as we have either expedited on some former previous earth-plane reincarnation, nor would we further impinge such philosophies as we have learned in these dimensions since our beginning and inception into these higher orders of spiritual understanding and learning. May I repeat that our service here primarily is to acquaint you with the functional nature of the various centers of Shamballa. Later on I will leave it to those who are more justly and aptly qualified if it is such a time and a place to do so to bring such philosophies into the plane of consciousness of the earth people. We here know that your earth is undergoing a spiritual evolution in which it will be a reversal from the great karmic plague of materialism as you are living under at the present time. Your great preponderance of superstructures of the materialistic world will gradually give way and be replaced by such spiritual concepts as will give a much greater peace of mind. However, for the present moment, Auka Makaula.

CHAPTER 49

Greetings, loved ones. I am speaking to you for the first time and using the transmission of the human vocal chords for some great period of time. I am known, and if I do not have too much difficulty with my earth brother's vocal chords, as Gamaliel. I was immediately preceded by my very worthy leader and colleague, Maha Chohan, who is the present presiding ruler or officer over this section of Parhelion, as he explained to you something of the concepts of reincarnation as they have appeared in the more spiritual concepts of the earth plane for some time to come. The past histories of your earth deal rather loosely and largely with the different concepts and translations, some of which are not quite factual. Other concepts are more relative, so it is our purpose to simplify and clear away some of the cobwebs of mystery and disillusion which are attached to these innumerable translations and concepts.

I believe Maha Chohan explained to you that there have appeared in your earth plane in the past several thousand years seven Messiahs or Buddhas, as they have been loosely called. We refer to Horus who was the immaculate conception, of Osiris, to the Jesus, to the Krishna, to the Shankara, and to one who was also known as Buddha in the northern China and Japanese areas. I believe that is seven, is it not? My pardon, I did not include him who you call the great

Manu who was also known by another name in another civilization which antedated any of your present earth books, one which was referred to you which existed in the northern Tibetan or southern Mongolian area something like a half million years ago. However, such as these Messiahs or Buddhas have been they have been working out through the countless ages of time their own destinies, their own reincarnations upon the pathway of truth so they might in the end evolve into such leadership of the Shamballas as they are now expressing. Well, it begins to look like I must learn to count earth time all over again. I did not include my very worthy colleague and leader Zoroaster who is known as Lord Maitreya. If you will pardon the necessary errors which may arise in such transcripts as we have contrived to be delivered to you, that these things must be delivered over the great vastnesses of time and space as your earth people call these various dimensions where we are expressing ourselves, that sometimes the element of error may enter into such transmissions. We here also, in these spiritual planes, do not claim to be free from error. We make mistakes just as you people do on the earth planes and as a consequence, we suffer some sort of, can I call it, karmic condition. So it must always be until we arrive at some ultimate state of perfection which is many eons and dimensions away from us at this moment.

Because we may appear to you as supernatural or supernormal beings who seem to glow or be on fire, this fact does not mean that we have gone beyond the time or place where such things as error do not enter in, also that these systems or histories and their relationship to your earth plane are tremendously complicated and require a great deal of research before they can be properly integrated into the concepts which will not be too confusing to the earth minds. Our problem here on the philosophical plane will be to explain to you some of the educational facilities and factors which we are teaching here rather than to explain any individual philosophies which may arise from the minds of such teachers and students who may be at the present time learning some of these facets or concepts. Now I believe for a moment we will rest until I gather together some more of the transmission and the power for its delivery.

Now that you have rested somewhat and gained your inner eye and some composure, let us begin to inspect this section of Parhelion which is devoted to the expression of the philosophical arts and sciences. As it is obvious that we are also expressing such services to a large group of the material planets and that such expressions are thus compounded in the functional orders here in these halls and classrooms, we will be forced by necessity, to avoid confusion, confine our explorations into such centers as are more directly relative to the earth plane of your existence. There is a great deal of system and order expressed here and indeed it is necessary that we do so. We have begun by saying that roughly speaking we divide our efforts or our expressions into such eras or epochs of philosophical science which relate to the periods of time of such renaissance of spiritual and philosophical philosophies that have existed on your earth planes from time to time.

Here is one large section which is devoted to the Chinese era. In going inside you will notice that like other similar rooms devoted to these purposes of teaching, that this also is of very tremendous or a very vast size. The ceilings are hundreds of feet high and are not ceilings in the true sense of the word. Just as they are in other centers of Parhelion, they are more composed of the radiant sheets of energy. The place resembles more what you might call something which would look like a large Chinese temple garden. Here you will see the places, the temples and various other structures which are related to the expressions of the philosophical arts and sciences as they were expounded in the ancient Chinese doctrines. Kung Fu often teaches his classes here although he appeared in the literary plane of a previous exploration because his work was necessarily compounded by such writings and transcripts in the written language of the ancient Chinese.

Pursuing our exploration somewhat further, we are now in a large center which is devoted to the Grecian renaissance of philosophy on the earth plane which existed some one thousand years before Christ and some several hundred years after Christ. This is, as you would naturally expect very Grecian in coloration and theme. We find beautiful Athenian temples and dwelling places in this room which have their Ionic, Doric and Corinthian sculptures very firmly and very beautifully typified in these numerous columns and facaded entrances which lead up from the marble steps and terraces into these various temples and buildings.

If you devoted so much of your time here for a few weeks, you might see such personages as Socrates or Plato or many of the other numerous exponents of the Grecian philosophies. We might also see some of the more modern contemporaries which have existed in your earth plane in the more recent or modern times. You might see Spinoza, Ouspensky, Emerson, Maeterlink, Wells and others who have lived in more recent times. I almost forgot Mme. Blavatsky. She is a very important figure in some of the classrooms in this section. She does not necessarily confine her activities in one relative classroom but seems to take great joy and delight in jumping into such breaches as are more necessary, and at that particular moment when a very pertinent question may arise, you may be sure Mme. Blavatsky is there with a very ready and quick answer. To you on the earth who know something of her biography, may I say to you that she has long since given up the practice of smoking cigars. She had to for she could not find anywhere where the weed was grown on this side.

Now here is a very beautiful classroom which is devoted to the Indian cultures and philosophies. Some of these were previously explained to some extent or to some reference in part of the previous transmission. However, I would further explain that as you see the very ancient cultural and philosophical backgrounds of the peoples of India as they existed for many thousands of years before the appearance of Jesus on your earth plane are here very aptly expressed in a pictorial setting of innumerable and various temples and other cultural centers. You who are interested in the great man called Mahatma Gandhi, (Mahatma, as you know, refers to some political leader and is the terminology of such leadership or expression) will learn that Gandhi has already made his ascension into this planet and into this center of Parhelion, because he was a very highly and developed soul before he made his appearance in your earth plane. A man who could control the thinking and destinies of millions of people, you can assume, was no small personage.

I would like to point out here that time, as the element of years in your earth plane as it has previously been explained, is entirely irrelevant in a pure esoterical transference of knowledge and wisdom into man's consciousness. It may be difficult for you to understand but in the ordinary sense an agnostic or an unbeliever or one who is steeped in the versions of the profane world, normally takes ten thousand years to make an emergence into some of our astral teaching centers such as Hermes or Muse, whereas in the case of a person as Gandhi who has so previously spent many hundreds of thousands of years in the celestial realms finds no difficulty in surmounting the barriers of time and space and almost immediately ascends into his true rightful position as a teacher and an Avatar in one of the centers of Parhelion. I would like to say that I have pointed this out more or less objectively with the view in mind that you will treat these leaders as they appear in your earth plane with a little more respect and decorum to which they are properly entitled.

Now we have come to another very large section of this teaching center of the philosophical arts and sciences. One is devoted to, and we shall call it, Egyptology. Here in going through the doorway, you will find yourself in something which reminds you of the great temple at Karnak or Thebes. At one time, if you study your histories of the earth more thoroughly, you will find that the Egyptians possessed a high degree of spiritual culture. I am not necessarily referring to the more degenerate or debased version which appeared in the later dynasties of the Ramses or such time as Cleopatra who sold out the empire of Egypt to the Roman minions. I am referring to the more spiritual or more aesthetic concepts as they were expressed before the time of Akhenaton. Going into the dynasties which existed at the time of the concepts as practiced by Osiris which was more monotheistic in its origin and belief, as that God or the Supreme ruling Power was expressed through the center of the sun, the Helios of all existence, as it warmed and revitalized in its daily cycular fashion through the succession of days as the great sun poured its energies and its infusions of radiant strength into the earth and to the many peoples. It was natural that the Egyptians and the peoples have from time to time worshipped the sun and rightly so. Helios is a representation of one of the great vortexes of celestial energy which pour down into the lesser planetary systems.

There are other sections of this teaching center, one which is devoted to a culture which existed in Ethiopia. Not much is known of this culture as it is written in your earth plane histories. However, there was at one time a very wonderful and beautiful culture in the country which is now known as Ethiopia. This was before the time of Egypt. I could go on and on and enumerate and show you various other historical sections which deal with these spiritual and philosophical philosophies as they have existed in your earth civilizations from time to time. There is even a section here which is devoted to and which exhibits some of the culture as it existed in Lemuria and in Atlantis and in some of the subsidiaries under which they exerted their control, such as the Mayan in your Central America, the Aztec or Inca who worshipped Quetzalcoatl and so on into an infinite number of other expressions, and then we need not stop at your earth plane but we could go on and on into other such similar planets and planetary systems and explore their philosophic and artistic cultures just as we have partially explored these which are relative to your own earth existence.

However, dear brothers and sisters, rest assured that in proper time and in such a number of evolutions, so shall the scales from your spiritual eyes be lifted away and you will begin to retain from your psychic and your Akashic the true memory consciousness of all of these things which have passed before you. You will begin to relate all of these experiences into a factual integrated concept of life. You will begin to understand things which are far beyond the realm of your very finite earth minds and which supersedes the bounds and dimensions which can be expressed in vocabulistic terminology. The nomenclature of your earth plane is not conducive to the higher expressions and so as you evolve you will drop these monosyllabic forms of expression and deal only with the pure esoterical consciousness which was explained to you as concept.

Down near the center of this section in what has been called the spoke, like in other sections, this too is devoted to the great galleries which we have called museums which also reflect into a more personal or Akashic way the histories of your many savants and philosophers of the earth plane as they have appeared from time to time. Like in the scientific section, these books too exist in a spiritual form of consciousness. As you saw and examined some of these works, they were unlike those in the higher astral realm of Muse that these books too will be found to be of a pure spiritual nature and radiate with the vitality, the energy and the spiritual wisdom with which they were propounded. It is the integration with the forces which you have termed the spiritual bands, the Guardian Angels of the higher and more fully evolved intellects as exist on your earth plane that such philosophical references can be very subtly impinged into the consciousness of the individual as he expresses his earth life.

To you in the realm and dimension of the material plane, about you there swarm the millions of your fellowman who are agnostics, we might say they are sitting astride a fence. They are neither on one side nor on the other. They are not sufficiently well educated or versed in the higher arts and sciences to form realistic convictions of their own, nor should convictions really exist. It is only the ignorant who become opinionated and biased in their expressions of life. It is unfortunate that from the ranks of these agnostics that many of the leaders in the more objective philosophies of your life sometimes spring forward and in the greed and the hate and the lusts of the world about them, they are continually exploiting their fellowman with the falseness of their doctrines. A true philosopher or one who is starting on his pathway of spiritual evolution will never say to his fellowman: "Only believe as I do or you shall not be saved," but rather, "Is there some small part of what I know that I may share with you that as you share with me, as we would our daily bread, we too can be nourished and sustained and revitalized by a new and firmer understanding of a spiritual philosophy."

It is well known among the peoples of your earth plane that people love a certain amount of delusion. One of the exploiters of the human race at one time who lived on your earth plane and who was known as Phineas T. Barnum and who is now evolving into a higher concept, expressed and capitalized on these emotional values of human nature. However, such delusions must come more or less with the conscious knowledge of the individual. He can thus tolerate a certain amount of delusion if he thinks he knows he is being deluded to a certain extent. It is only a deflation of his ego if he becomes deluded in the unconscious sense and awakens the following day to find that his delusion has been very real and that as a consequence he has suffered. This is karma in one of its many and countless forms as it is incurred in the various and numerous translations of life in the earth plane. However, I see that as a philosopher to some extent naturally and inherently, I have been straying somewhat from our true course as we walked along these various passageways, until we looked about us and gained something more of the perspective and view of these vast and immense centers of teaching.

Around you, you see there are numerous students and teachers who, like in the other sections, are coming and going about in their various duties and activities. All seem to be tremendously interested, very vital, very radiant and very much alive and full of health. If you were to stop them and question them individually, you would find them coming from the various other sections of Parhelion, or they may be coming from the higher astral planes or worlds such as Muse, as teachers or students in their various interrelated facets and understandings. Through, all and about you are the continual streaming pulsating Radiant Energies. Yes, it is a beautiful place here just as it is in many of the others, although the accent is on simplicity. And while there are many wonderful and beautiful statues, carvings and works of art that you see interspersed at frequent intervals along these corridors and hallways, there are also wide places where great fountains of energy are playing from some unseen and unknown source. You may think them wet to look at, like the water upon the earth planes, yet you could walk through them, brother, and you would emerge perfectly dry on the other side. Your only impact would be to feel a tremendous pulsation or throbbing sensation as you walk through them. Such as it is, these energies are very often used for revitalization and the renewal of the pulsating energies which you see stemming from our various centers in our psychic bodies.

Many questions seem to arise and while we are on the plane, little sister, (Ruth asked mentally regarding his previous statement of the energy fountains from an unknown source) my ears can hear your voice too. No, there are no unseen forces if we look objectively enough. The Radiant Energies, as they stem from the fountains and in other various ways and other expressions, do have an originating source which is, roughly speaking, the Divine Fountainhead. As these energies are, in themselves, very intelligent, they express themselves in many, many ways and that it is our purpose here as was explained in the Venusian transcript that we learn to live, to direct, to use, to become part of and to function with these Radiant Energies. So, until a further visitation, your true friend and brother, Gamaliel.

CHAPTER 50

Bon soir, mon ami, and to my beloved fellowman on the earth, my fondest greetings and salutations. I am Rene Descartes, a Frenchman who lived on your earth plane in about the 15th century, somewhere in the time of William Shakespeare; and welcome to our planet of Hermes. You have somewhat explored the innermost workings and the halls and various classrooms and functions of the center on Parhelion in what is related to the philosophical phases and concepts of your earth life. As I spent a lifetime in a somewhat recent period of your earth history, I am teaching some classes here in the central city of Aureleus on our beautiful planet of Hermes.

Now I believe a word here about philosophy and its various respective factors would be of some value in forming a more cohesive thought pattern in your ideas and relationships to such philosophical planes of expression as have been in existence in various times in your earth planets. Philosophy itself, as you have discovered with other elements of these teaching centers such as art, does not mean an artist daubing paint on a canvas or a scientist working with a test tube but philosophy, like many other of the concepts, is very firmly interwoven with the other and numerous facets of life. We can say in a broad sense of the word that philosophy enters into everything which is about you on your earth plane and you shall in your evolutions and reincarnations to come, not find the time and place where philosophy does not enter into such facets and concepts.

Yes, we might say even the bird and animal life as it exists in your planet has certain philosophical aspects. We could say that the bright-eyed little bird who lives in the tree next to your doorway has his own philosophy which makes him an incurable optimist. He is concerned only with the worms he may gather for his food or to watch over the eggs which his mate may be sitting on in the nest. Philosophy can be said to be roughly the adhesive substance of mind which links or relates the different aspects of man's nature into such relationship as makes life in some plane or in some expression more conducive to a fuller and conclusive development.

About a twenty-five hundred years ago in the land of Greece, there was ushered in at that period and time the Hellenic Age or the age of philosophy as it relates to the more modern histories of the world. In the succeeding hundreds of years, many of the great and foremost thinkers and philosophers who have existed in the period of our history gave the fullest concept and measure of their knowledge and wisdom at that particular time. We have named some of these philosophers such as Socrates, Archimedes, Plato and of course there are a host of others who are not so familiar or so well known. Most any doctor can tell you of Hippocrates, the father of medicine, or Pythagoras who is the exponent of the various forms of numerology. It was Plato who expounded the first theories of reincarnation as they relate to your more Western world ideas of such spiritual evolutions.

There is a distinct separation in all of these philosophies from such Eastern world philosophies as they were more adapted to the Western way of thinking. However, the basic spiritual concepts in either case were somewhat closely interwoven. Shortly after the resurrection of the Avatar Master Jesus, there sprang into existence the beginnings of what was to become two new and very powerful churches. From a schism of a church which started from the Christian histories of Jesus, there sprang into existence from Paul, the foundations of the Greek Orthodox church and the Roman Catholic church. Thus it was that the history of Europe for the next many hundred years became one in which the destiny of mankind in the European countries became completely suppressed in an ecclesiastical form of tyranny. It became unlawful and punishable by death to speak or to live except according to certain preconceived lines of thought. The head of this ecclesiastical church held the key to heaven and hell for every human being under the many countries of its jurisdiction. This great ecclesiastical order also held within its hands most of the combined wealth of the countries and nations. They elected the various governmental heads and factions. They even controlled the actions of kings and queens.

It was not until the time of Martin Luther that any single individual ever succeeded in breaking loose from the closed confines of this dogmatic ecclesiastical order. Others had tried this, but had met with such burnings and other forms of torturous death, on the wheel and through hangings and various other public executions. Yes, even Dr. Harvey, who was a friend of Bacon, met such a death because he expounded his theories of circulation of the blood. And so here was the first serious attempt at a liberation of thought and purpose in the destiny of mankind.

After Martin Luther, others came along who made such similar contributions to freedom of thinking of mankind. Beside Bacon and Harvey, I played some small part in such liberation and freedom. We had others who followed in the years to come, such as John Wesley, Wycliffe and many others gave some form of philosophical and religious freedom to the masses of people of the world. However, much of this has been written in your history books and I would not wish to be accused of being repetitious or to confound and confuse you with such historical facts as have already been propounded by the learned men of your planet.

Before we actually engage in exploration of the city of Aureleus in this planet of Hermes, I would like to explain something of the theory which was expounded in reincarnation or evolution by the Grecian philosopher Plato. It was Plato, as I have said, who brought the first constructive ideology of the perfect order and sequence of conception which is called reincarnation to the minds of the intellectuals of the Western world. To those of you who have started on the pathway of truth, a little more light cast upon this subject would perhaps be in order. So let us begin by assuming that some individual is starting at the very beginning of his evolution.

We will say that there are three initial steps, which must be first taken before he is ready for the fourth step or the step of consecration. These three initiations or steps relate to the carnal, to the mental and the spiritual nature of man. They have also been called the working counterpart of the triad. So it is that the individual will reincarnate many times into such planes of expressions in the physical world which will relate him to these three basic concepts of his evolution. By the time he has passed through the carnal into the mental states of consciousness, he will find himself emerged into a spiritual state of consciousness which will focus and crystallize his ideas and his ambitions into a spiritual dimension which will enable him to take the first of seven more basic evolutions or reincarnations which will bring him to the place of his first spiritual initiation.

Throughout these seven basic fundamental cycles of his evolution, he will reincarnate from time to time into the higher astral worlds of Shamballa and to such centers as Muse, Hermes or Venus or to such other relative planes as will be further described. It is in these centers he will learn the more basic fundamental concepts of his evolution as it relates not only to himself but to the races of mankind in general. We may assume that he has started in his evolution in the consecrated effort of music but to enable him to become a musician he must also learn of the many other different concepts which enter into the production of harmony or tones as it can be expressed in such works as symphonies or other orchestrated forms. He will therefore in these higher astral planes of learning of Shamballa, relate himself and pass through the various seven centers which are so related to his original basic concept of music as it was expressed on the planet of Muse. There he will not only go through the initiations which will enable him to travel freely about through the five different centers but he will also in time through the seven basic fundamental cycles have so evolved through the other seven that he will have formed a very basic and fundamental concept of his particular profession. Thus it is that he has become a spiritual initiate. It was such spiritual initiates as were expressed in your earth plane who were called by the names of Mendelssohn or Beethoven, Brahms, Bach, Wagner and others who have been named in the musical world. We here have named some of the initiates who have been in the philosophical world. You have also been told of many of the initiates who have existed in the scientific realms and dimensions.

These seven basic cycles will take the average person about ten thousand years to complete in a normal relationship of time as it is expressed in years on your earth planet. After this spiritual initiation, he is thus enabled to ascend into the center of Parhelion where he will again start a new cycle or evolution of seven basic cycles which will take him through the seven centers of the city of Parhelion. Each of these cycles will take anywhere from about one thousand to three thousand years to complete. After he has emerged from these seven cycles, he is then a Master. Such a normal course in the passage of time in your earth years would consume something from fifteen to twenty thousand years of normal spiritual progression. However, there have been many initiates and Masters who have consumed three or four times that amount. They have also reincarnated into the spiritual planes.

It must not be assumed that anyone who reads these lines can lay down for himself any pattern whereby he can say in his curriculum or format of education in the spiritual realms that he will pass through such planes and initiations in a natural order or sequence as I have so described them. These are factors which vary considerably in the case of each individual as to how much karma he may pick up in some of these evolutions. It also may be determined by such factors which he himself will wish to express in the relationship of learning. He may also wish to reincarnate innumerable times into earth plane dimensions to further strengthen and solidify such concepts as he has already mastered. So it may be that he may consume a hundred thousand years or even a longer period of time before he comes to the point where he can be considered a Master and a teacher in one of the centers of Shamballa or to such other associated centers as may exist in other galaxies or in other universes.

So in the sum and total, it might be said that after you have spent a great many thousands of years in the physical or carnal planes of the earth or into such related earth plane consciousness which are even of a lower rate of vibration than your own earth, you may evolve into the state of consciousness where you will dedicate yourself to some spiritual purpose as it relates to the more beneficent expressions of your relationship to your fellowman. You will be fired and consumed with the idea that there is much to be learned, and much to be expressed and much to be taught. Thus it will be that you will have taken your first step of initiation.

It is only at this point that you will begin your gradual climb into the spiritual realms of consciousness, into these dimensions which we are describing to you. There is no hard or fast rule which can be said to determine the actual time or sequence of the various factors of reincarnation or evolution as they are determined by the basic fundamental frequency concepts or relationships of these frequency concepts which relate to epochs of time and to such other fundamental factors as are involved in the nature of the individual himself. These factors are largely determined by his own consciousness and by his own strength of purpose and also by the wisdom which he has acquired and in its proper usage and proper function.

We may say roughly that such reincarnations may occur at such regular intervals of three hundred years or six hundred years or nine hundred years and so on. Usually we find such odd figures or factors entering into such concepts. If you will study the works of Pythagoras, you will find the basic relationship of the number of twenty-one which, as I have said, it means that it is something like twenty-one thousand years before you are an initiate to the centers of Shamballa.

Now something about the planet of Hermes. We can be said to be something of a similar nature or structure to the other planets which you have visited and that as you come into the city of Aureleus proper that it is in a general way somewhat familiar or reminiscent to these other centers which you have visited. Here again there are the all-pervading Radiant Energies which you see in abundance about you. The planet itself, as you have come into its immediate vicinity, seems to throb and pulsate or to oscillate in some strange manner with a variety of colors. The overlaying or predominating color here, however, was green. This is a very soft and soothing color as it is related to the aspects of understanding in your earth plane. Here, however, the transference of energy in its particular frequency vibration spectrum assumes somewhat different proportions, as has been previously explained.

Coming down into the city proper, here we find as in other teaching centers of Shamballa that this also is indeed a vast and a tremendously enlarged place. You have nothing in your cities or civilizations on your earth plane to compare with the magnitude of these cities. They seem to stretch out in all directions around you. As we further investigate what these cities are and to their various functions, the city of Aureleus itself is said to be divided into a large number of sections, each one somewhat along the manner which was previously described to you and which you saw in the third section of Parhelion.

In other words, we have a large cultural center of

396

Hellenic or Athenian art and culture which relates to the philosophical sciences. We have also the Chinese section and here also you will find the students and teachers or initiates which were at one time incarnated into your earth plane existence in the country of China and Japan, and this center is particularly Mongolian in aspect. You will also find many other centers in which the architecture and the outlines of the buildings are very strange and unfamiliar. These sections relate to other earth-plane dimensions which as yet you have not explored and with which, you are not too familiar. You may have at some time evolved or incarnated into several of these spiritual planes but as yet in the psychic condition as you exist, you have not retained any fundamental memory concept of these centers.

I sincerely hope that I have made this exploration and transmission sufficiently intelligible to be translated in your present earth plane language. Here in these centers we use a universal language and as you have no doubt surmised by now that it is somewhat difficult to transport the factors of concept as they exist here into the vowels and consonants with which you are familiar. However, you will return for a visitation to Aureleus and you will be guided about into some of the centers so that you may obtain somewhat of a better perspective of the many facets and working parts of this great center. Until such time, may we wish you the abundance of God's all-permeating intelligent radiating Wisdom into your innermost being.

CHAPTER 51

A fond greeting to you, friends. This is Friedrich Nietzsche. I was of German origin and extraction in the most recent of my earth-plane reincarnations. I have been somewhat elected to help conduct you in your next tour of our city of Aureleus.

There has been a rumor on your planet for some time since my demise that I was somewhat mentally unbalanced at the time of discarding my fleshly envelope. It is well for some to say things about others when they do not understand what others have been doing or of what their work consisted. If this was insanity, I only wish that many more of your earth plane people had the same condition. Your world would not be in the position in which it is now. It might be said that many of those who have contributed to the posterity of mankind in his many relationships and facets of endeavor have at some time or other been called crazy. You have slang phraseology which you use now in your earth world about you, such things as 'having things loose in your heads', however, I will not take up any more of this precious time by such references.

Rather, let us begin the business at hand to explore this section of Aureleus, which as you see is somewhat reminiscent to you of the pictures you have seen of medieval Europe at about the time of the 15th or 16th century. Here you see the architecture which is predominant at that time fully expressed in a very highly evolved state which is as in the case of other centers and planets all of the Radiant Energy structures. You see English-style buildings of the Tudor construction or motif. You also see German style villages which seem to be thatched with the straw or hay of the fields. You may also see great cathedrals which remind you of the cathedrals which you might see in France or in Germany. We have not here in this city gone to any lengths to construct museums, as we have made, shall I say, full scale models of the various philosophical eras of mankind upon the earth. You might wander about this city for many, many years and see the different centers which are devoted to the architecture and the style of living as it was expressed in that particular time.

We could go back to the beginning of Chinese history in some ancient Chinese village and see life as it was depicted at that time and that era. We might see a cross section of Egyptian culture and philosophy as it was expressed in some of the homes and temples of ancient Egypt or that we might go into India and see there too how people lived in the most ancient of times. Yes, even a cross section of the period of Atlantis and Lemuria are also here depicted, so that all of the races or philosophies of mankind are truly illustrated into such a factual manner as best befits its time and its place, so that the student may in his own selected relationship or field go directly to such a center and spend such time as he so desires in the constructive elements of his philosophy.

In the few works which I left upon the earth plane, much of the more abstract concepts of evolution of man's nature were entered into. Some of these have already been explained to you by some very worthy colleagues in the other centers of Shamballa. As it has been explained, we do not personally interject such philosophies of the nature which were expressed in these earth-plane relationships. Rather, we are individually expressing a collective philosophy which relates in a relationship to mankind in general as he exists at your time and your place on the earth planet. Such obvious gaps or flaws in the philosophies and nature of man are thus constructively pointed out so that the obvious and necessary changes may be made.

Our nomenclature or terminology is by necessity limited somewhat and is further tempered by the discreet use of such words as will bear more of a harmonious relationship to such people as may be tempted to peruse these different writings.

In strolling about this center which was somewhat related to my own time and my own existence as I lived somewhat later than my colleague, Descartes, who gave the previous transmission. However, the progress of man is slow to change, so we might say that in this center we will find all of the elements which entered into the era of time of Europe which was not only his period of working out a new freedom and liberation but also indirectly led into some of the darkest and blackest pages of earth's history. In this center as it portrays the elements of that period of history, you will find many of my worthy colleagues who are teaching some facets of the philosophical sciences to many and various students who come and go through these centers. You also find many teachers who are from other planetary systems and from other planets of which you know nothing. Such relationships here as have been explained are for the purpose of more correctly integrating these various and numerous facets.

As no student or teacher is in his reincarnations limited to one particular planet, he must before he has assimilated the necessary sequence or consequence of such numerous evolutions, have gone into numerous other planetary systems and will have mastered to some degree the necessary portions of his particular science from these relative planetary systems. We hope very strongly that many of the individuals who will read these pages will be so stimulated that they will read some of the works of the various personages who have given some of these transmissions. We sincerely hope also that such works as we have so contrived will be of some value in further liberating the consciousness of mankind in the earth plane as it exists at the present time.

You are indeed much in need of liberation for your own age has produced its own chains of bondage. These are not ecclesiastical in nature but are instead a great and gigantic robot, a mechanical robot which is like a juggernaut from which the crushed bodies of millions of people are strewn about the earth planet. And I will say, not only are the bodies crushed but many times the souls also suffer. Until such further transmissions, may I send you the very best of God's Rays and energies of Love.

CHAPTER 52

Greetings, dear ones. May the Prince of Peace always dwell within your house. This is he whom you call Gamaliel. It is at this time that we will resume our exploration of the center of Shamballa which is dedicated to the philosophical sciences as they existed in the many planets such as the earth. But come, let us go directly to the great city of Aureleus and thus begin somewhere where we left off in our previous transmission. As we approach the planet, you will see that like many of the other great centers that it too is of an immense size and that it seems to spread out for many miles in all directions. However, we are more concerned with the structure which you see just before you. This is the great teaching center of the many philosophical sciences. Like all of the others, this too bears some similarity. The atmosphere here, if we can call it such, is the pulsating Radiant Energy with which you have become familiar. The planet itself bears somewhat of a resemblance to your own earth planet, inasmuch as the over-pervading color seems to be somewhat of a greenish tinge or cast. The great central structure which you see before you which is the teaching center of Aureleus, is too, constructed of the crystalline materials. Here, however, the greenish radiance also seems to be very predominant among the very beautiful auric colors which stem from these structures.

In the center of this vast circular building is a huge

temple which like the one on Parhelion can seat several hundred thousand people. The huge dome-shaped roof stretches on up into the heavens above to a height which would eclipse your tallest skyscraper. But come, let us sit on the temple steps for the time has come when the creation of your earth must be explained to you.

As it was foretold, the mysteries of heaven will be unfolded and that man shall come to a newer and fuller realization and understanding with the creative forces of his earth planet. In your Bible as it exists on the earth plane, you have the story of the creation and it is thus said that there was a great void of blackness and that God said, "Let there be Light and there was light". However, this is not quite factual. To the physical eye of the unbeliever and the unbeholder, there would be a great blackness and a great darkness of the void which is called space, but to him who discerns with the spiritual eye, see-eth just as you do in your spiritual consciousness, the great permeating radiance and brilliance of these energies which solidly fill the space and which is called void or space in your earth conception.

A more factual illustration of the creation of the world begins with the Will and Intelligence as it is so conceived by the Immortal God, Father or Central Vortex or Fountainhead, as it has so been called. Thus it was so ordained that your earth should come into existence because it would serve the necessary purpose in the evolution and reincarnation of countless thousands of your fellowmen. As it was explained by Faraday in another transmission that in these great voids which are called space, there began the cycular motion of these Radiant Energies as they portrayed the fullest intelligence of the Infinite Creation from whence they sprang.

403

In this cycular motion and in the forces which are somewhat likened to the centripetal forces or motions which were so explained, that in the course of the many ages or epochs of time, a great, hard-core nucleus was thus formed of the negative wave forms which were precipitated into the center of this great vortex. Your sun was so formed, so was your earth. So the thirty-three Logi who watch over these many and innumerable earth planes, such as your own, had so directed and so conceived this vortex of energy should become the earth planet. It was they who charged the twelve Lords or Archtypes who thus were so intelligent in their various effectual orders of equation that they directed these energies into the semblance and form of the spherical globe on which you now reside. In the course of the many eons of time, the energies so rearranged themselves into the elemental structures as you know and call them by their various atomic equations as elements. And so it came to pass that in the many ages as your geologist has so described as Eocene or Pliocene or Carboniferous or such other of the forty-three ages which he has associated with the formation of the earth crust, and that in all of these layers of the earth's crust, were laid the many treasures of the earth which were necessary and so preconceived that in the evolutions of time as man appeared upon your planet, he would so need these various and innumerable treasures of the elements for his daily life.

Thus it was that the great stores of petroleum and coal were laid beneath the surface. The great treasures of iron, of aluminum, of copper and of many other of the earth elements as you know them as metals or minerals were so stored in the vast treasure houses in the crust of the earth.

It so came to pass too that as it was partially

explained in the principles of evolution by a colleague by the name of Darwin that in the natural evolution or sequence of the various types of life that abounded upon the surface of the earth as it gradually materialized into your physical consciousness that these species would reincarnate and thus regenerate themselves into new and different species, and thus was evolved the concept of your physical body as it would function perfectly in such a dimension.

Darwin, however, neglected one principle and although he was a very spiritual man, he did not stress emphatically enough the infinite and intimate nature of all creative forms of life on your earth planet as they were so conceived in the higher and more relative spiritual dimensions from whence they came. Now you are beginning to see and form within your mind something of the form and thought as it was so conceived in the Infinite Mind as to the creation of your world and of the plan which God had for the races of mankind which would in the future ages live upon this planet. We will for the present moment neglect any forms of life which were relevant or pertain to the general structure and characteristics as they related to man in the earth planet and go directly to the origin of the earth conception of the Shamballa.

Through the many ages of existence of man through the thousands of years, there have been references to this mysterious Shamballa and its existence in the southern Gobi desert or that in some such place there was some great holy city of supernatural splendor and brilliance. Now you earth people have a quotation something like, "Where there is smoke, there is fire", and as there has been much smoke, we will see just exactly what the fire is like. We will thus start our story somewhere in the chronology of the earth about a million years ago. At that time the earth had so developed on its outer exterior that it could now support the higher and more advanced forms of life and that the time had now come when man in his entirety should be firmly planted upon this earth. And so it came to pass, with the Venusians working with the twelve Lords of the earth as they had been so relegated and dedicated into the services of your planet, that they came in their great space ships and that the other planets of the more highly evolved spiritual nature also came with their various artisans and craftsmen and so that in the hundreds of years which came to pass they erected from out of the crystalline structures and transmuted them into your low earth plane dimension a great and huge crystalline plateau many thousands of feet high in the center of the great Gobi desert.

Upon this vast plateau or plane was actually constructed this city of Shamballa. As it existed at that time and that age, it too was constructed of the Radiant Energies and was divided actually into seven different parts which properly equated each of the seven dimensions as they are in the seven astral worlds of Shamballa above them. Now as this great plan progressed and many races of mankind evolved in their reincarnations as spiritual counterparts into this city of Shamballa, there taking their proper initiations, they again reincarnated into the physical flesh and became part of the tribes of people who lived upon the surface of the earth around and about this great crystal plateau.

Here they too came into some sort of spiritual abundance and that it might, in some way, parallel the aspects of the Garden of Eden. However, the Garden of Eden is a pure parable or allegory and should not in any way be construed with any life as it existed upon your earth planet. The Garden of Eden merely refers to the original spiritual concept of man and that as he reincarnates into the earth plane he has begun his actual evolution as a biune being or a being of two parts and equalizations as male and female. Such beings are ordained and preconceived purposes of Infinite Mind. You have long confounded yourself with this very simple allegorical equation and you have misconstrued it from its true spiritual meaning and purpose. However, I see that I have digressed somewhat from my original explanation. Getting back to our story, we see now that we have the beginning of a great and wonderful race of humanity as it exists upon the reaches of the earth surface about this great crystal plateau.

It was not a desert in those days but bloomed and blossomed with the profusion and abundance of all the most gracious blessings which were capable of being bestowed upon it by the higher dimensions. It was a veritable paradise in a pure and simple sense of the word. Man found life simple and uncomplicated. It was easy to procure food and he lived easily without crime and without the carnal lusts and desires which are so prevalent in your world today. And so in the thousands of years time, it so came to pass that now it was necessary that man was to be born into his own physical world without the guidance and help of the spiritual Shamballa which had, up to now, protected him somewhat and led him in his earth-plane existence. And so gradually the great Shamballa was dissolved and absorbed into the reaches from whence it came.

In the many generations which followed in the earth life of these many tribes of people who abounded around and about in this part of this great world, they came to know not the existence of this great spiritual center of Shamballa but the legends and tales about it still persisted in their minds and memories and were handed down from generation to generation. These people became in the final end the great Aryan race which descended into India at about a half million years ago and became the forefathers of the seven root races as they exist on your earth plane today.

And so it is through the countless thousands of years which have passed since this time that they have laid down the foundation for all of the spiritual concepts and racial attitudes of mankind as he exists upon the earth plane today. It is not my intent or purpose at this time to explain these different concepts as they are tremendously vast and complicated in themselves. It is my purpose here to take a shortcut as it were to explain to the minds of the earth people so that they may clear up some of the confusion which has resulted from the innumerable and multiple explanations of the origin of man.

We do not confuse these origins of the seven root races with the Chinese and the Japanese. They are, in themselves, a migration from the planet Mars and as they arrived on your planet hundreds of thousands of years later, they carried with them a more pure and a spiritual form of a basic concept which has existed in the land of China even unto this day. To the many races and cults as they exist in India today, they too had their concepts and origin in the Aryan race as it came from the northern reaches of Tibet and southern Mongolia from the tribes of peoples who were thus left behind from the epoch of Shamballa. A rather rough summation of these seven root races would be to say that there is the Brahmanistic which is, of course, vastly complicated and assumes a multiplicity of forms and various and diverse creeds, cults and caste systems, Brahmanism, Hinduism and other such forms and expressions which are all somewhat related and dependent upon the higher form or Brahmanistic concept as it exists in the priesthood of India today.

We can also say that there was the Persian or the Arabic root race which was the ancient Chaldean. Another important branch which came from the Aryan race were the Egyptians, the Ethiopians, the Latin races, the Teutons, the Nordic races and the North American Indians, so that in all ways and in all manners of speaking, their original customs and racial characteristics had their basic concepts in the original Aryan race. It is our purpose on this exploration to further explore some of these more basic or divided root race concepts as I have just outlined them to you. We will go into the various sections of this great center of Aureleus and there you will see the integrated concepts which are being taught into the plebeians and initiates as they come and go into this vast center. However, for the moment may we rest.

Again, dear ones, we have just somewhat discussed the creation and the placing of mankind in his evolution upon your earth plane and that our most recent discourse as it concerns man in your immediate evolution or environment started something like one million years ago, and while this all seems very simple and very easy to do in a few minutes time, you may rest assured that if you will think for a moment that it involves things which are beyond your imagination. The innumerable concepts, the races, the civilizations which have sprung up and ceased to exist, many of these have not even been written in your earth history. In the jungles of India there are civilizations and cities which lie buried which would give much to the relationship of your earth-plane concept of man as he has existed from time to time. I would like to point out to the earth scientist and to those who may be so interested that you may think that in your present day that your atomic science is of a new origin but such is not the case. In the ancient temples and in the various religious centers of India as it has been written on the walls and in the sacred writings, the scientist would find interpretations of atomic structures which would be far in advance of those which he possesses today. The same is true in the ancient lore of Egypt. Even Hermes had a much better association of atomic structures than your more advanced scientists.

So it was, these ancients had their knowledge and wisdom of atomic structures and their relationship to the Infinite source or energy Fountainhead as you have called God, and that in the understanding of this relationship, they could appear and disappear, that they could perform the innumerable and countless wonders which have been whispered as legends or have come down to you through the ages of time in more factual forms. We can say in the most recent portrayal of such science was that which was displayed by the Avatar Jesus and that He walked upon the water or walked through solid stone structures with the apparent ease of walking upon the surface of the earth and that these things have not yet occurred to you that there might be something indeed to the written and unwritten pages of history which you have not heretofore examined. It might be well for you to pause in your wild and mad flight in some fancied realm of atomic disintegration and to seek a more earnest and sincere evaluation of the spiritual values and concepts which have been entombed in the various places of the surface of your earth. Even you have so basely misconstrued the spiritual concept of the origin of man as it has been portrayed as Adam and Eve into some sexual malpractice that is not factual, and is entirely irrelevant to its original spiritual interpretation.

My brother has just given you something of a dissertation or a factual explanation of the origin of the various races of mankind as they exist upon your earth planet. I shall therefore go on with this transmission. I am Maha Chohan. He has given you something which you may best understand as to the many and different mysteries of the sciences and philosophies of your earth plane. It is well to remember at this time that all these things present something of an improbable paradox inasmuch as we are actually, as it was said, making a camel pass through the eye of a needle. In this case, you are the eye of the needle and we are the camel. We have not attempted at this time to go into a very complicated explanation of the factual orders of the different theosophies and theologies which have stemmed out of the migration of the Aryan race from the Mongolian plains.

Suffice to say to the student who is interested, that your earth libraries contain much factual information on these subjects. Such exponents of the occult and theosophical philosophies of life were somewhat gone into by my colleagues such as Mme. Blavatsky, Ouspensky, Churchward and many others which at the present moment and for the sake of time, I will not attempt to mention.

There is one point I believe was not mentioned which I think would be rather relevant at this time to explain. At the beginning of the influx of the Aryans as they came from the north into the southern plains of the Ganges of India and that as they carried with them the traditions, the legends and theosophies of their race that they came under the protectorate of one who is called Manu. Later on Manu may take charge of some future visitation into some future center of Shamballa. It has been so devised and conceived in the Higher Minds that the earth planet is at all times under complete jurisdiction of such spiritual forces as will best regulate the cycles of time and the expressions of mankind which exist upon it. You may think that you are creatures which are dependent upon the products of time and evolution but this is not entirely so.

Such evolutions and the products which are involved in the transmission of these evolutions and involutions of reincarnations are preconceived purposes which are born from the original desires of mankind himself. We here who have evolved into the higher planes of spiritual consciousness so nourish and further stimulate the natural sequence of these spiritual evolutions as to the betterment of the various races of mankind. Such is the infinite and ultimate purpose of the great and emanating wisdom which comes from the great Central Vortex. In some short time we shall resume our exploration of Aureleus, the city of philosophical science and my worthy brother Gamaliel, shall take over. He begs your forgiveness for the interruption. However, until such time as he again resumes contact, may the Radiant Energies of God's Love permeate your entire being.

CHAPTER 53

Good morning, dear ones, this is Blavatsky. As I am quite well known to you on the earth, I shall not waste precious moments by discussing my own personality. As this subject in this chapter is very close to my heart, I begged to be the one who would conduct you in your next tour. Philosophy, as you know on your earth plane, to the individual becomes the code of ethics whereby he conducts himself in his daily life. Collectively, to a nation of people, the conglomerate philosophies of all the people become their political systems and their religious conduct. Roughly speaking, we may divide philosophy into three different categories: the physical or material which pertains to the expression of life in the baser and more elemental concepts, the mental, which is so expressed in his business affairs or into such professions which abound in your cities and such other and numerous associated expressions, the spiritual philosophy which man has expressed, the most dominant and the most vital to his progress. It is the spiritual philosophy of a nation which guides its destinies so that it either becomes a great nation or that it passes into the oblivion of time.

Before we enter directly into this large city and into the section which is particularly devoted to the ancient theosophical or occult cultures as they related to the beginning of the Aryan race of mankind, a brief digest of what has formerly been given would be in order here. As you were told, the Aryan race was planted upon the earth for a very obvious reason, that as in the future it was to become the seven root races of the numerous civilizations which have been so vital and pertinent to the history of your planet, inasmuch as these people, in themselves, were forming the conclusions or particular sections of their involutions and evolutions through the many reincarnations.

Shamballa, as you know, began about a million years ago in your time. However, do not pay too much attention to such chronological statistics as may be given to you as such appearances of time in your earth planet are rough summations of such occurrences. Time, as you know, assumes a different factor and perspective in our dimension. Shamballa was the net and conglomerate efforts of the seven Shamballas in the higher astral spiritual dimensions, combined with the efforts of the numerous Lords and of the thirty-three Logi who rule our particular dimensional system. This was a very beautiful city as it existed on the great crystal plateau in the southern central section of what is now known as the Gobi desert in Mongolia. Through the many thousands of years, there came into being numerous tribes and races of people who surrounded the mountains, valleys and plains on this wonderful and beautiful land. Under the direction of these Lords of the earth, the land was very fruitful and brought forth a tremendous abundance of all of the necessities of life for man as he existed in these numerous places about this great Shamballa.

However, the time came when the spiritual evolution of the earth was such and that the vibration, shall I say, changed to such an extent that it was necessary to remove Shamballa from the face of the earth. And while this was done somewhat in a spirit-

414

ual fashion, yet the final conclusion was such that it was like a great noise and a fire and wind which swept down out of the skies and carried away part of the earth into the heavens. Now as you have also been told, this Shamballa was constructed of seven different sections which functioned in direct relationship to the seven sections which are being explored by you, in the writing of this book. This is the basis for the legendary tales which are still in existence on your earth plane. If you will remember your school histories and that such men as DeSoto and Cortez chased these imaginary seven cities across half of your fair America into what is now Arizona to try and find these fabulous legendary seven cities. There are also numerous other stories which pertain to these legendary seven cities, however, as you now know, their true origin is the Shamballa.

One of the very striking disclosures which will be made in this book is the numerous references to the Old and New Testament of your Bible and of the parallels in the numerous stories which have entered into its fabrication. One of these stories relates to the casting out of Satan out of heaven and that he descended upon the earth with his hordes of angel followers. The true origin of this story began during the time when Shamballa flourished upon the earth and that Satan was an actual person in the form of a man who was called Brahavada. He was later called something else but to simplify matters we will call him Brahavada as he existed at that time. He became a very powerful leader in one of the numerous tribes which surrounded the Shamballa and as he grew in power, he became an insurrectionist and revolted against the spiritual dominions of the Shamballa. So he was banished, and taking his numerous followers with him, he migrated down into the southern part of the Asiatic continent which is now known as India. With the passing of many thousands of years and with the disappearance of the great city of Shamballa, the time came when the Aryan races as they existed there were confronted with a new and very vital problem. With the passing of the spiritual age, the land began to dry up and become desert-like in appearance so that they were forced to begin migrations to seek more fertile lands elsewhere.

One of these migrations which took place, began several hundred thousand years ago and swung around to the north through the country which is now known as Siberia, and into Russia and through what is Finland, and became the Nordic or Teutonic races. As the original Aryans were very blond people, they were tall and of good stature, had ruddy complexions, blue eyes and light hair and they preserved these racial characteristics in these Nordic or Teutonic races. Another of the migrations which began carried them southward into the more fertile plains of the Ganges river basin into southern India. It is these peoples of whom we are more vitally concerned at the present moment. They have long ago forgotten much of the Shamballa and that it existed only as the various gods and their spiritual concepts. In emerging into the Ganges plains, they found a race of people who had formerly been driven from the original place of Shamballa. These were called the Dravidians, a very proud and haughty race who tried to keep themselves from mingling with the Aryans who were also a proud and haughty race.

Now it so happened that these Aryans had three basic concepts somewhat along the philosophical lines which I have previously described. It was in the frictions and interminglings of these two basic tribes of people which gave rise to the caste systems as you

416

know them in India today. It was the trying to keep apart from each other which later developed into the four castes. Now in order to save a bit more time here, we will neglect for the present moment the more complex structures and the different factions of gods and goddesses who entered into the Brahmanistic, or which was later to become the Buddhistic concepts of the Indian races.

At the early beginning before the time of the Gautama Buddha, these religious systems resolved themselves into three dimensions—the Brahmanistic which had its origin in their Brahava, the God of all, or the Great One or the All Pervading Source. The second division was the Vishnu. This related to the more mental perspectives of life on the earth plane such as was symbolized by the sun and of the many beneficent blessings which this particular God bestowed upon the earth. The third, which is more generally prevalent and well-known in India today is called Shiva. It is this faction which relates the Indian people to the baser and more elemental perspectives of their religions. Such innumerable types of self-imposed punishments which they undergo are part of this ritualistic expression. In the earlier concepts, much of the sexual aspects of their religion was entered into from the god Shiva. In the evolutions of time, such other sundry divisions have sprung into existence, such as Jainism and an innumerable number of such smaller divisions which would, in itself, be a lifetime study. At the present day there exists a nucleus of the original Dravidians who have become mentalists and lexicographers of no mean reputation and have adhered very closely to their original concepts through the countless thousands of years. It was the Mahatma Gandhi who in your time freed and liberated India not only from the yoke of the British but also from much of the pressures of the caste systems as they have existed through the ages of time.

Now that we understand how it actually was that Satan was cast out from heaven. Let us progress further in our discussion and enter directly into this section of the city which is devoted to the culture of the Indian races as it existed from the Aryan invasion. Here you will see historically depicted a vast and numerous number of temples, shrines and other such edifices and buildings which were characteristic and typical. Many of these buildings are actual counterparts of the original structures as they existed on the earth, except that here too like everything else, it is all crystal. I really like these crystal buildings. They are very pretty, don't you think? Now, however, they also serve a more utilitarian purpose and that all these various temples are also used as classrooms for the various students, initiates and such other people who come into these places to study the religions of these races of people. Progressing farther along in our tour we shall also begin to enter into other sections which relate to the excursions or the migrations of the original Aryan races into other parts of the world such as the ancient land of Syria or Babylonia as it is depicted in your history books.

Other migrations took place into Egypt and into Greece, Arabia and into other lands that were around the Mediterranean area at much later dates. It is from the pre-Babylonian, the Hittite and the various phallic cult systems which existed in that country from which much of the origin of your New Testament has sprung into origin. In your history books and your Bible, it tells you that the Jewish people were captured by the hordes of Assyrians and that they were brought back into captivity into Babylonia. It is here that they learned many of the stories such as the one about Satan, the flood and Noah's Ark and many other stories which I could name at this time which were later interwoven into the fabrication of the New Testament in a different form.

It was at a much later date that here too in the ancient land of Persia and in the country of Media that a great spiritual prophet was born into the world by the name of Zoroaster and that he came into life about a hundred years before the Gautama Buddha in India. You will also find in consulting your history books that in ancient Babylonia and before that time that they too had a Moses who was found floating in the bulrushes and who was later raised in the temple and became a great king and leader of the people. The name of Zoroaster himself conjures up one of the enigmas and puzzles which have entered into the spiritual philosophies of the earth plane inasmuch as he too was a son of immaculate conception being conceived from mother earth by the Ahura Mazda who was the God of all.

The Zoroastrian theology later on became the foundation for the Mithraism as it existed in the Mediterranean countries and that such concepts were entered into as the Spring Festival of the Vernal Equinox and the slaying of the bull or Taurobolia, which was later, in the time of Paul who became the founder of the Christian churches, interwoven as the ascension.

Now I see though I am getting ahead of my story somewhat and that we are getting ahead of our place here as we explore this city. Here we have finally come into a section which is devoted to the ancient and the more modern Egyptology. Here you will see the civilization of Egypt in some small way depicted in the numerous temples as you see about them. Here you will see an actual small-scale model of the great temple at Karnac in Thebes and thus this Egyptology will be explained to you somewhat by the numerous books which deal specifically with this subject on your earth plane. We might start with the time of Osiris as he existed about twelve thousand years ago on the earth plane. He was actually a migrant priest from Atlantis and he came into Egypt to teach the fundamental philosophies and concepts of the spiritual religions as it existed from the higher planes of Shamballa. Osiris later became, through the passing of thousands of years, a legendary figure or a great god who was the keeper of both heaven and hell. It is the story of Osiris which also has the strange parallel to the resurrection and the immaculate conception such as is depicted in your New Testament. It was Osiris who overshadowed Isis, the mother of earth and conceived Horus who corresponded somewhat to the story of the man Jesus.

Later on in Egypt a great Seer and mystic arose by the name of Hermes who collected much of the ritualistic forms as they existed at that time and compounded them into a great science which was later somewhat depicted in what is commonly called "The Book of the Dead" which is not the book of the dead at all but actually means a way of life.

In the beginning of the Osirian era, Osiris taught the separation of the spiritual consciousness from the physical body or trance as you know of it now and that such people who have separated themselves could travel in the spiritual dimensions for any length of time they so desired, returning in several weeks or in several months, and there in the temple they would write in their books the knowledge and wisdom which they had learned in the higher dimensions. It is also truly said that at the end of the Osirian Age that a hundred of the priests or initiates voluntarily entered into the lower astral realms which were closely connected with the earth plane and that their bodies were suitably embalmed or wrapped as they were in a suspended state of animation and that the bodies were very closely wrapped and sealed in waxes and gums and that they remain hidden in a deep subterranean cavern to this day. It will be part of what is called the Second Coming when these priests again re-enter into their bodies and manifest themselves to the earth people. Meanwhile they have been working closely with the various nations of the world for the good and the advancement of mankind.

Now we shall slip somewhat rapidly and go into the more, shall I say, modern times such as the Hellenic or the Athenian period of time which was immediately before and after the appearance of Christ. There too you have been somewhat made acquainted with this particular type of the philosophical age or the renaissance as it was termed. Some of the foremost thinkers of that day in their numerous types of science were somewhat alluded to or mentioned and I will not further complicate the pages of this book by such explanations as I might give as many of these philosophers of that time are quite unknown to the earth people. I would like to stimulate their curiosity to such an extent, however, that they would look up in their encyclopedias and read somewhat of this race of philosophers, poets, historians and other people who worked in the expression of some philosophical science. It is from the foundations of many of these philosophies that we have today some of the basic concepts of your present civilization in the fields of not only philosophy but in the more scientifically related fields.

Now I see we have come into the section of this center which is devoted to the Hellenic or the philosophical expressions of that age and of that time. Here we will examine some of the things which are more pertinent to that time. We will begin by these large charts or diagrams. These were originally conceived by an astronomer and astrologer by the name of Ptolemy who was the personal adviser to Alexander the Great of Macedonia. Here you will see by close examination of this chart that he so conceived that the earth was the center of the universe and that the seven planets revolved around the earth and that the stars or the universe was on the outside of this system.

Now getting into the more advanced types of astronomy, we will see here some of the diagrams of Plato and that now the universe is heliocentric with the sun exactly in the center with the seven planets revolving around and that the stars or the universe is on the outside of this. This was further enlarged upon by Copernicus and I might say that each one of these various Athenian philosophers had their own particular concept of astrophysics. It was not, however, until the time of Galileo and the advent of the refractory telescope that a more complete freedom and liberation into the astrophysical or astronomical realm was entered into. Galileo, as you know, was the Italian who lived at about the 14th century and suffered much indignation and persecution for his advanced philosophies and science.

Another parallel to Galileo is a little Dutchman by the name of Leeuwenhoek, who made his first microscope and explored the submicroscopic realm and entered into the consciousness of man a full and complete new dimension which later became the foundation for your medical science. This medical science incidentally had its beginnings as far as your earth is concerned in its modern interpretation, with a Hellenic interpreter by the name of Hippocrates. However, after the time of Leeuwenhoek, other men reincarnated into your earth plane with more fundamental concepts of the science or philosophy of medicine.

Here again your history books will fill in much of what I cannot give you here, such men with whom you are more familiar—Pasteur, Koch, Lister and numerous others most of whom are here studying in the various centers of Shamballa. Now you will begin to see that even after the burning of the great library in Alexandria, and while this can be truly said to have plunged the civilization of the earth into the dark ages for more than a thousand years later, yet at the beginning of the time of Martin Luther and of others of such mental stature that it was indeed the beginning of a new Age and as you will think more closely, it begins to assume the proportion of an Infinite plan, which it truly is.

We here in the numerous centers of Shamballa before and after the time in which I took my place among them, have been long working to guide and direct the destinies of mankind in his evolutions or epochs of time in the earth plane expression, such as it is necessary and has been so directed by the higher Angelic Kingdoms from those who are the Logi, the Lords and the Archangels who preside over these terrestrial dimensions. Now until such further discussions, I remain your true and sincere friend, with all of our love, Blavatsky.

CHAPTER 54

Greetings, dear ones, and welcome back to Aureleus. I hope you have forgiven my sudden disappearance. A small crisis had arisen with a group of students in the temple who were taking the initiation. I believe in your previous tour that you were conducted by my dear colleague, Mme. Blavatsky. However, there is much in this particular realm of philosophy which requires a good deal of study and that I believe we shall start somewhere in the beginning to let you further examine the temples which are contained in this section of the center of Aureleus. Now stretching out before you is a long corridor or avenue. On each side are the various temples and other edifices or altars which depict or denote some specific teaching or are dedicated to certain gods or to such aspects of both modern and ancient religious and philosophical beliefs in India. We will step into the first one which happens to be at the beginning of this avenue.

As you enter the doorway, you will see at the end is a great figure of the god Brahma, as he was somewhat depicted in your earlier tour. He is being drawn in a chariot across the skies by the seven Rishis. By now you will have guessed that this temple is dedicated to the teaching and explanation of the earlier Vedic cultures as they were expressed in the Aryan migration into the southern planes of the Ganges in India. Now on your right hand side is another huge statue of a god known as Vyasa or Vishnu. He is the preserver of Life and the Enlightened One and con- tributed much to the earlier concepts and well-being of the spiritual welfare of the people of India. On the left hand side is another depiction of the god Shiva. It is he who depicts much of the material or the carnal structures of man's nature. In his doctrines are expressed the philosophies of Maya or the illusion, and the Yoga or the self-punishment in which various torturous dogmatic creeds were entered into. It is from these concepts which flourished in India for many thousands of years which gave rise to the very strong caste systems.

Now let us pass along this avenue and enter an- other temple before which you see an immense statue of the Gautama Buddha. It was Buddha who taught a direct contradiction to much of the earlier Brahmin- istic beliefs. It was Buddha who taught against the caste system and that strangely enough, there is much in the writings and teachings of Buddha which have a very strong parallel to those of Jesus. The disciples of Buddha wrote the three 'Pitakas' or the gospels. There were also Ten Commandments of Bud- dha. It was Buddha also who taught his disciples to go forth to the masses and preach the truth. Jesus said to his disciples, "Go forth and spread the Light" and so it can be said that of this Master who lived five hundred years before the time of Jesus that he did much to free and liberate the Indian peoples from their earlier animistic beliefs.

I believe that in your previous tour that you also touched somewhat into the Zoroastrian concept and into the Egyptian. Mohammed, however, was some- what neglected as was the Hebraic or Judaism. As both of these religions are quite well known and widely spread on your earth today, a little discussion might be worthwhile at this point.

Almost everyone is familiar with Mohammed who in his earlier youth became a camel driver and later on married the woman who owned the caravans and as she was wealthy, this gave Mohammed much time for meditation. It seems that all great instigators or leaders who develop some new cult or ritual on the earth plane have always at some time seemed to have talked to God. So it was with Mohammed. After a trip from the desert, it was he who declared himself a prophet and that he had talked to God and set up what later became the religion of Mohammedanism and although Mohammed could not read or write, he dictated the Koran to his disciples which became the word of life and philosophy to millions of Moslems. However, much of this is in your history books and I will not waste time by further explaining or by confusing you with such further explanations. We have temples or mosques here in which the students can go and obtain factual knowledge of the religion of Mohammed in the comparative evaluations and the philosophies of the world as they are taught here in Aureleus.

The Hebraic religion also was quite neglected and for an obvious purpose which you shall soon see. We intended to surprise you if we can in some small way and this is being done as you will see in a moment. Now we are stepping out into a large courtyard. Before and around you is a great esplanade of a beautiful mosaic tile. Directly in front of you, however, I see your eyes are riveted on the temple which you see before you. This is somewhat different than any temple that you have previously seen inasmuch as it seems to be square and that the walls are rising in a tapering fashion to a huge beautiful dome-shaped roof which sets somewhat back from the edge around all sides. This temple, like all others, is constructed of the translucent crystalline material which is so familiar. I see in your mind there is some sense of a vague remembrance to a picture previously seen of the Temple of Solomon on your earth plane and such as this is which is the Temple of Solomon. It was the wise Solomon himself who as a direct psychic manifestation actually reproduced with the earth materials the Temple of Solomon in the Holy Land.

Now come with me and we shall walk into the great central courtyard and we shall sit a moment and watch the passersby, the students and teachers who are going about in their various pursuits. The actual history of Judaism starts somewhere back in ancient Chaldea about two or three thousand years before the advent of Jesus. It was Abraham who led the Jewish people out of Ur or Chaldea into Egypt. Now at that time Egypt was flourishing and engaged in a tremendous program of expansion. In those days much of the activity was determined on the manpower which they were able to produce. The Pharaohs, or kings usually produced this manpower as the other emperors in history, by going forth and making war on other nations and driving back the poor unfortunate captives into slavery, such as it was in Egypt. It is said that Abraham was bargaining in a labor market with the Pharaohs to produce enough labor to help erect some of the temples and pyramids which were at that time being undertaken. Both the Pharaohs and the Jewish people were very clever tradesmen and so as it developed that in the hundreds of years the Jewish people almost overran Egypt and so the Pharaohs turned about and made war upon them and drove them into a large enclosed city where they remained for many years. It was during this warlike interlude that a truce was set up

427

whereby the Jews bargained for their liberty by producing enough labor to set them free. So in consequence, they were in a form of bondage or slavery up until the time of the appearance of Moses. With the advent of Moses, who was half Jewish and half Egyptian, it came about that much of your Biblical history was portrayed. The seven plagues and the various other different magical or psychic manifestations which appeared to haunt the life of the Pharaoh and the Egyptian was finally culminated by the Exodus.

Now Moses was a very wise man in many ways. The staff of Moses has become the caduceus of the Jewish people. It was he who in his clever knowledge of astrology was able to lead his tribesmen to the borders of the Red Sea at the particular moment that a great comet passed very close to the earth and drew the waters of the oceans away from the Red Sea, so that he was able to pass with his people dry shod onto the neighboring shore. I would like to point out that much of the phenomenon as it is portrayed in miraculous stanzas in your Bible have been such divinations by seers or other such holy men who have been able to predict the occurrence of some astral phenomenon. Such was the case of Joshua and that the so-called stopping of the sun was actually the appearance of another celestial body which lighted up the earth and enabled Joshua to completely decimate the armies of his nation which were opposing his own armies.

We can say that the history of the Jewish people has been divided into three periods or epochs: the period of Abraham, the period of Isaiah, and the period of Solomon. After the advent of Jesus, the Jewish people and their power declined from its zenith and passed into oblivion of history as today they remain just the remnants of a once proud and mighty race of people. And so in the future as you may as students study the Bible in both the Old and the New Testaments, you will see and this will somewhat explain to you the strange parallels of many of the things which you will see there which actually have their advent or their appearance in some previous religious or theosophical expression as it existed in some other nation at some other period of time. Much of that which is in the Old and the New Testament as so portrayed in the many and various stories which have been accepted literally and factually are actually based on many of the legends which came out of Assyria and Egypt and were borrowed in the various ages of time and written into these histories. From the Aramaic, from the Babylonian and from the Egyptian philosophies and theologies, we will find the origin of many of these stories. They were intended in the beginning strictly for spiritual or philosophical interpretations of some viewpoint or aspect of life and were not intended to primarily convey a factual interpretative happening as it may have actually occurred. Now I believe I will pause a moment while the mistress makes certain alterations. (A new tape was needed on the recorder and immediately he was aware of it.)

Now that we are again in order I will continue. I mentioned being somewhat suddenly circumvented in a previous transmission. This was because of an initiation ceremony which was going on at the present time. Although the temple as you see it before you and its great courtyard seems to be apparently without such manifestations as ceremonies or other things of public nature at the time, yet beneath this great temple is actually in progress an initiation ceremony. For some obvious reasons, I will not be allowed to take you into these lower halls and classrooms as this ceremony is now in progression and is of a very highly secretive nature. We do not like to lay down the lines of demarcation and have tried up until this point to explain to you all of the mysteries of heaven and earth. However, there is some of this which cannot be possibly given to the earth people at this time, as if it were so it might lose much of its value and factual meaning to the individuals if it were so explained. So for their sake, I will refrain from actually visiting these chambers that you might see what is in progression.

You have on earth at the present time an order of people who are called the Masons. Much of the Masonic rituals have been derived from such initiations as are in progress at this present moment. There are some thirty-three orders of Masonic initiations and that is a very highly evolved spiritual order which was conceived primarily from such expressions as are taught in these centers of Shamballa. It is therefore to protect this order that nothing more than a partial explanation will be entered into. We might say that the initiate as he has passed through certain initiations in other centers and in various earth-plane reincarnations is in such a position to become what is sometimes called an Adept. In such a position he will come here to this great temple and at a proper time when such ceremonies are in progress, he will take his initiation.

This is done usually in three steps, the first step which is called the Maya or the Illusion. It is here in these chambers that for some period of time the initiate will go through the stage of temptations. He will actually live one or more lifetimes in the course of a few hours. He will be tempted and sorely tried by the many visitations of earth temptations. These will assume a seductive female form or he may be whirled into a maelstrom of such influences which may

430

seem to him to give him world power and dominion over the masses. These illusionary dreams may be likened somewhat to those which are incurred in an opium smoker in the dens of iniquity which flourish in some of the earth cities except, of course, that these illusions are of a much greater and of such a nature as they may embody a number of reincarnations. Should the initiate succeed in surviving these numerous temptations, he will then be in a position to go into the second.

It is here in the second that he exercises the power and dominion over the mind. He will be able to factually display the projection of the mind forces and how the mind can be used to catalyze the various energies which are in existence in these beautiful centers of Shamballa. He will, in a sense of the word, demonstrate factually that he has succeeded in evolving into such state of mental consciousness that now he would compare with something like a man who visited your earth two thousand years ago. We refer to Jesus.

The third initiation is strictly of a spiritual nature and involves such concepts and principles which would be very difficult for the third dimensional mind to grasp. It also embodies such concepts as exist in higher realms and dimensions and with such Logi and Archangels that it would be extremely difficult to portray even a small portion of this initiation ceremony. We can say for short, that the initiate actually travels into some of these higher celestial spheres and that he will undergo such tests as are duly contrived by these higher forces.

Now there is, of course, much more in this great center of teaching and learning in Aureleus which we have not fully explored. There are such great halls and museums which relate to the more familiar or the more modern philosophies and theologies of the earth as they exist at your time. You may enter hallways and museums which are devoted to such exhibits which relate to the Athenian or Hellenic Age as it existed before and after the advent of Jesus. You may see many of the old pantheon of Greek gods as they were very accurately depicted by a comparatively modern English historian by the name of Bulfinch in his "Age of Fable", and so I will not digress or further confuse those who will read these lines by such a vast and what might be a repetitious consequence of such explorations. I will therefore leave it to the individual to further fill in such details which his imagination may best supply and I may need not say that it is not necessarily his imagination for while he is reading these lines he may very well be prompted with such spiritual forces as will properly institute these concepts to a much greater and fuller degree.

I may also add in my concluding transmission here with you that all of those who do read these lines, should fully remember that they will be thusly initiated into a higher order of understanding than any in which they have previously so incurred in their various evolutions. My one regret is that we could not more fully bring to you, more individualistic expressions or to the many and numerous teachers and students many of whom have existed on your earth plane in some reincarnation. We have tried in some small way to explain to you that in the principle of reincarnation we see a great and combined intercourse of peoples and nations throughout the many and thousands of terrestrial planets in the universe.

It has so been contrived that in the evolution of your earth that there is much which will have to be eliminated, much will pass away and in consequence, much will be added and much will be renewed. These will be spiritual concepts of which man knows little or nothing about at the present day. Many of these age-old philosophies, which you have been seeing and which have been described to you, will in consequence become mere historical fragments of the existence of the earth planet. It has been the greatest pleasure that I have been able to conduct you through the center of Aureleus and to explain to you some of these factors in the elements of philosophy. There is in the future for you much work to be done. There will be other sections of Parhelion to investigate. There will be other planets to visit. In the future there will also be many more books to be written but until such time, we will wait upon the pleasure of the Infinite Spirit of God and may He reside and express Himself in the fullest measure in all the moments of your life.

Gamaliel.

CHAPTER 55

This is your most humble and obedient servant, Lao-tse. I have had the great honor conferred upon me of conducting you on your next tour through Aureleus, so we shall begin immediately in the section of this great teaching center which has been devoted to the philosophical expressions of Chinese culture, both ancient and more modern. As you will see stretching out before you, something which seems to resemble a vast and beautiful Chinese city except that unlike the earth cities, as it is constructed of the same beautiful crystal energies, that it is glowing and pulsating with all of the colors of the rainbow. As we wander down this fair avenue, you will see on either side a vast assortment of Chinese temples, pagodas, beautiful gardens, fountains and arched bridges across the many streams and lakes. These are all of the ancient and more modern Chinese architecture. While these structures here relate more to the actual teaching activities of the Chinese philosophical cultures, yet you will find on the outside of this teaching center another section of Aureleus which also was of the Chinese culture wherein lived many of the old sages and Chinese exponents of philosophy.

It is somewhat with sadness that I am entering into these discussions as I have looked into the earth China and have seen the great disseminations that have been wrought by the pagan gods of communism.

The ancient temples have been desecrated and turned into brothels of iniquity. The Chinese people themselves are sorely troubled and perplexed. They cannot easily accept a new ideology which is foreign to their nature after living for so many thousands of years with their old gods and beliefs and expressions of the ancient Chinese philosophies.

As you look about you, you see before you some of the great temples, huge and immense statues, several of which look like the Buddha statues of Kamakura in Japan or that they may represent other statues of Buddha as he existed in the various histories and temples of China. So let us pause a moment here and look about us and reflect into the wonders and beauties of man's spiritual nature.

We who are the Chinese do not claim to be one of the seven root races while in a broad sense we may have been included in such theologies from the earth plane expression, from such earth plane philosophies as have been previously discussed, yet in an absolute concept as it was so brought to you at another time, we were migrants from the planet Mars and we came into existence on this planet well over a hundred thousand years ago. The earth geologist and researcher has long been confused with the element of time in his studies of the ancient races of people and that he has not yet fully evaluated such circumstances as time. It is quite obvious that many of the old and ancient writings would in such extensions of time pass into oblivion and would thus have to be reinstated with newer documents or other historical representations.

In the beginning of our history on the earth as it was explained to you by Nurel (the channel's Martian guide in the book, "The Truth About Mars") that as the great space ships in our intercourse with the planet Mars established a series of six colonies stretching from the lower planes of China into the more northern reaches around what is now known as Peking in the provinces of China. There was in existence at that time descendents of the Aryan race who lived as Mongols or Tartars, as they are called in your history books. These were mostly very fierce roving bands of nomads who roamed the now desert regions of the Gobi desert. It is with these races of people that the original Martian settlers had so much trouble. As in your Martian philosophies, it was obvious that these people had progressed to the point where they disliked intensely to kill their fellow beings and while they had weapons to thoroughly and completely decimate these nomadic tribes, yet they refrained from doing so and relied more upon the evolution of time as would be of such circumstance that these tribes would absorb some of the wisdom and knowledge. However, this was not so. In the numerous raids which they made upon these settlements, they frequently captured both male and female prisoners and that as the females bore children to these Mongols and Tartars, we became somewhat infused into the racial characteristics of these people. However, for the most part, the various dynasties of the Chinese empires can be traced directly back to the Martian line.

As it has been very apparent to you from the numerous pages of Chinese history in your modern philosophies that we have been a people who were for many thousands of years a race who devoted a great deal of our culture to the more spiritual natures and concepts, and so it is that we have had a great deal of gods or goddesses who resided in our homes and in our temples. It is further illustrated that there were also great dragons. I would explain these dragons as something which were similar to the Biblical version of the serpent in the Garden of Eden and that our dragons also represented certain evil forces. You may also have questioned us as to being heathens and worshipping idols. No, the Chinese do not worship idols. The various ceremonies, obeisance, etc., which the Chinese individual displays before these gods are very similar to such expressions as are entered into in the Christian ritualistic services. In one of the very large Christian churches in your modern America, you will see both old and young bowing down before such statues of the Virgin Mary or of the Jesus and that while they are not actually worshipping these statues, yet they are appealing to these persons as individuals, in a higher esoterical sense, is this not so and as we do also in our worship to our various gods or goddesses? Thus the great Gautama Buddha was also worshipped, not as an individual but with the spiritual virtues which he so represented. In the more ancient China it was a land of great happiness and much peace and while there were at different times great conquerors who came in to plague us and that it was so we had to, at different times, build walls for protection against these Mongol and Tartar invaders, such as the Genghis Khan and others. He was the son of a great conqueror and was the Khan at the time of Marco Polo and his father who entered China at about 1200 A.D.

In our homes just as it was before the invasion of the red Communists, there were many of these gods so depicted which represented the forces of good and Light which you have symbolized by such saints or personages as have existed in the Christian dogmas and creeds. Some of these gods are quite familiar and have been characterized in numerous reproductions in the American philosophies. There is one in particular, a small, round, fat, squat personage who represents the element of happiness and joy. The names of these—I see that I have aroused some difficulty in translation into the American dialect and so I will more or less leave it up to my brother and sister if they so desire to interject the names of these various gods into the lines of this work. However, this is not entirely necessary as most people will know what I am talking about anyway. (Ho-Tso, pronounced Ho-tye)

Ancient China, through the many thousands of years in which it flourished, was a very wonderful and beautiful place to live. The farmer who with his wife worked in the rice paddies with his bare feet and in the water, sang the songs of his ancient ancestors or that it might be so that he constructed his humble dwelling with the bamboo poles and the thatched roof of straw and even though he was in, as you may call it, poverty of material possessions and often slept with his chickens and pigs, yet he was supremely happy in raising his family of sons and daughters, nor did he have any of the conflicting elements which are found in your present civilization. He did not worry about the income tax and among the hundreds of other taxes and complications of your political systems. It is sometimes that he so farmed a portion of land under some lord or ruler of a province and that as such a farmer he would often pay a small portion of his rice or other grains and products to the lord. However, such taxation was usually not nearly as oppressive as the taxations which are in your present civilization.

For many thousands of years the Chinese knew of gunpowder before it was ever known in Europe. They knew of many other different things too, such as the production and manufacturing of beautiful textiles which were produced from the fiber spun by the tiny silkworm at about the time of Buddha who lived at one time in China as he so reincarnated into this land from another plane of consciousness. With the passing of Buddha, there were others who came into China who stole the secrets of the silkworm culture and they were again reproduced in India and Borneo and in Turkey and other countries, so that it was before the time of Marco Polo that the fair ladies of Europe often wore the silken raiment and garb which was produced from the tiny fibers of the silkworm.

In a very pure or relative sense, it might be said that the ancient religions of China before the advent of Buddha were of such nature that they were comparatively simple. The temples where various votive ceremonial observances were so performed were usually in such related facets of man's life as they were immediately concerned to him. If it was so that a woman wished to conceive a child, she would go to a certain temple and lay upon the altar her offerings to a certain deity who would intercede in her behalf and thus she would so conceive a child. Or it might be that the husband himself would wish to offer a votive offering to some great deistic personification which would also bring rain and the abundance of the harvest, so that he too would make votive offerings unto the altar of some temple.

The art of China itself is, as you will see if you visit many of these great temples which you see about you, just as it exists in your museums and in the various other more modern expressionistic endeavors of the present Chinese people; it is extremely intricate, very beautifully fabricated whether it is of the ceramic type which is known as china or in the fabrications of cotton, linen or silk. Just as on Mars today, the Chinese people express a great deal of patience and extreme care in the fabrication and construction of all things which they do. The secrets of such things as lacquers have long remained hidden from your modern chemist, nor can they be duly duplicated as these secrets of chemistry were handed down to the Chinese from ages and ages ago. To see a beautiful piece of Chinese art such as an embroidered or a mosaic screen is, in itself, a revelation of artistic beauty and that as these artistic sciences are nowhere duplicated on your earth plane, so it is quite obvious that we, in ourselves, possessed at these various periods of Chinese history something which was, in itself, unique and far different than anything which has heretofore been expressed on the earth plane.

You may question why Kung Fu did not make this exploration with you, however, as you know that he conducted one in a section of Parhelion which was devoted to the philosophical science of literature and that as Kung Fu was himself a collector of such works and philosophies as related to the many hundreds of his fellow countrymen who were so engaged in expressing various concepts in the philosophical sciences which related to life in China.

I would speak a word here about the cultures of Japan as they existed in the past and in the more modern times. In Japan the religion of Buddhism has not been so strongly expressed and that it has been in direct competition with other more materialistic expressions of philosophy which are called Shinto in which the Japanese very often very loosely worshipped some collection of godistic expressions in his earthly life. However, there are masterpieces of work in the Japanese temples of the Gautama Buddha which flourished there somewhat in the same time as it did in China proper.

The Japanese are an offshoot of the original Chinese race who migrated and became separated from the continent or mainland through a great earthquake. As it was explained in your transcript from Mars, a great celestial body passed very close to the earth at a period of about one hundred thousand years ago and great changes in the geographical locations and placements of continents took place on the earth's surface just as it did on Mars and other planets in our solar system. Before that time, Japan was an integral part of China, so was Formosa and some more of the other lands which have sunk beneath the sea. After the great cataclysmic passing, the geography existed much as it does today. I might also say that previous to that time there was a great difference too in the climatic condition as it existed in China, in Mongolia and Tibet. Previous to that time, it was a much more moist climate and produced a much greater profusion and a luxuriant display of vegetative masses of plant and also great numbers of animals which have long since passed into the oblivion of history.

There is in the history of China and in the northern provinces stories of the great mastodons which used to come down from the northern reaches and invade the villages and raise great havoc. The mastodons have been perfectly preserved in the great masses of ice which exist under the tundras of the northern reaches of Siberia. Such flesh as has adhered has been preserved in a perfectly frozen state for over a hundred thousand years. An explorer or two of the white race have made excavations and have so eaten the flesh of these mastodons. It is also with great sorrow when I say that the great red pagan god has also invaded Tibet and has also taken Tibet over. I will say for the benefit of your political leaders as they are trying to build a wall of China around this

441

great red pagan god that they will not be entirely successful. India, too, is to be in the future taken over by this great red pagan god, likewise will be Burma and many other countries such as Thailand. With the passing of Chiang Kai-shek, the Chinese Nationalist leader as he is on the earth plane today will also see the end of Nationalist China.

You will in the next twenty or thirty years see such differences in the geographical separations of your continents into political systems which will resolve into two great nations in direct opposition to each other and such it will remain until a future time when the new and seventh root race makes a greater and fuller appearance than it has at this time. The seventh root race is the spiritual race which is making its ingress into your planet at this time. There are many leaders of this race who are already in existence and are forming various nuclei in the different countries which will in the future manifest a great deal of liberation and into the spiritual policies which will conduct the destinies of mankind on your earth plane. So until such future time as my very worthy brothers may come in and conduct you into such future tours, may I say to you that may you always be bathed in the Radiance of His Most High Presence.

CHAPTER 56

Greetings, dear ones, this is Maha Chohan again. Now I believe in view of what has happened, that it is a very appropriate time that some of the higher orders and equations shall be given to you as you were so properly led and guided that some of the further mysteries of heaven may be explained to you. I believe you have been made aware that there is actually a small planet or asteroid named Eros which is in the consciousness of the earth mind astronomer and that the existence of this asteroid is somewhat known in the scientific circles. To avoid confusion, this is not the true spiritual planet of Eros. This smaller planet which will be described is an asteroid which is somewhat smaller than the moon and in the rate of frequency vibration as it exists in the spectrum, exists somewhere between the high astral orders of Shamballa and the lower earth plane orders of terrestrial planets.

This small asteroid is something like a half-way station or an Ellis Island or what you could call a customs service inasmuch as it functions in the service of your planets of the solar system whereby the Initiates or Adepts who have just recently completed their reincarnation in some earth life and have emerged from the flesh always go to this sub-planet of Eros. There they are conditioned in such relative factors as will change their vibration or that will cleanse their psychic bodies of the taint of the lower earth planes. They will also undergo such severances which will separate them from the close ties of family relationships which are somewhat overstressed and are quite needless in the higher orders of the understanding of vibrationary communication. An Initiate will go to this sub-astral planet of Eros and as he is thus conditioned, he may remain for several days or he may remain for several years depending quite largely upon the individual and to the relationship and how it is that he is functioning in, in that relationship.

This asteroid, as it has been properly guessed and evaluated by the earth astronomer, is a cylinder but it is more than a cylinder; it is a seven-sided cylinder. Each one of the facets relates itself in a certain frequency spectrum connection with its own respective section of Shamballa. We might say that there is a beam of energy which shines from one to the other which makes it possible for the individual to very quickly communicate with the proper portion of Shamballa in which they are to reside.

This asteroid, in itself, also makes an orbit. It is a true orbit of an ellipsoidal shape or like an egg. At one end of this orbit, it comes in very close contact with the earth and with Venus and Mars. At the other end it extends on out into the planetary systems so that it will contact other of the more remote planets such as Neptune and Uranus. Thus you see it performs a very useful service and function in the proper orientation or segregation of the different initiates or individuals who have lived in these various planets from time to time.

Now this orbit, as it revolves around, has also been closely evaluated and that it actually takes thirty-six years to complete, thirty-six years of your earth time. In the opening transmission from Eros, Nikola went into somewhat of an opening discussion of an orbit which he described as nineteen hundred and thirty-six years. This is not pure coincidence as far as your earth time is concerned. The orbit which he referred to had its understanding or concept in a much higher plane of relationship. If you will properly understand, time as it exists in these planes or dimensions is entirely different than your earth conception of time. If you live on the earth for thirty-six years and transferred that thirty-six year period into living on Eros, you would actually live for thirty-six hundred years. What I mean by that is that you would evolve or that you would learn and you would progress, you would otherwise assimilate and render your services unto your fellowman the equivalent of thirty-six hundred years that you could do this same service and this same educational work on your earth plane. I believe that is clear; is it not? This also will now explain to you that as Nikola meant, the turning of your century which was 1900 and that the next close parallax of this planetary orbit from the astral planet of Eros would occur at 1936 and 1972 and so on. At the conjunction or parallax of each of these orbits, you will find if you will trace your history very closely that there were some particularly significant happenings of the earth histories at that time. At the opposite end of this parallax you will also see that there was somewhat of a recession of certain spiritual and scientific values as related to your earth planet.

The recession of our cycle was 1936. Shortly after that Hitler began to rise in power. Thus you see it was that while we were the furthest away from your physical planet in our physical vibrationary impact that the dark forces succeeded in pushing their way into your world in a much stronger relationship. So it will be in 1972 that here again we shall be in close conjunction with you and that again you will find a recession of the dark forces and a new impetus given to the spiritual and scientific factors in your dimension. Now you will also begin to see why there was some information which was somewhat of a nature which might tend to confuse you in the opening transmissions from Eros because this subject, as you have now determined in your own consciousness, is very broad and very vast.

Also a previous transmission which I would like to clear up and I believe was not made properly clear was the evaluation of the soul's individual progress as it was explained from the Platonian concept of ten thousand years. Here again we will refer back to a few moments ago and will multiply the 10,000 by 100. Therefore you will see that your soul progression has now assumed one million years if my multiplication serves me correctly. You will also refer back to the time when we told you that the Shamballa appeared on the earth almost a million years ago. This, in itself, is a very significant cycle inasmuch as it is now closing. In other words, the Shamballa is to appear again on the earth plane in a spiritual form. This means the Second Coming of Christ or the rebuilding of the City of Jerusalem, whatever you would like to call this spiritual age, as it is revealed to you in Revelations as the building of the City of Jerusalem or as the Second Coming of Christ.

So you will see that we here in Eros and in the other cities and centers of Shamballa will actually come into such relationship with the earth plane that it shall know a spiritual age which has superseded anything which is possible for you to now envision. However, the full impact of this spiritual age will not be immediately realized. We mean by the turning of the 1972 period of time that as this parallax will be expressed in the earth plane consciousness that it will be somewhat of a revival of spiritual values and scientific relationships. But this, in itself, does not mean that the exact conclusion of the one million year cycle has culminated. The actual conclusion of this cycle will occur around about the year 2000. It will be from that time on that your earth plane will know the meaning and the true value of its spiritual impetus and its new awakening into the realm of the Second Coming or the new re-establishment of the City of Shamballa upon the earth.

Yes, I may truly say, brothers and sisters, that the great beautiful crystal structures of Shamballa will in a future day actually live on your earth again as they did a million years ago but you will not see them in your time. Perhaps some of the very youngest generation which is being born into the world at this time will be enabled to envision the actual coming of this great spiritual age and this beautiful City of Shamballa but it is even beyond that. So do not chastise yourselves mentally by feeling that you are to be cheated from seeing the appearance of the Shamballa because it is truly known that in your own spiritual progression, you will evolve and revolve into the earth plane consciousness for many evolutions to come. You who are initiates or have even become shall I say, adepts, have yet to work out many reincarnations which will involve not only your earth plane but the many planes which are associated with and under the direct spiritual guidance of the Shamballa.

We here know of these truths and of many more and as that we too know of this Shamballa and that as we are describing it to you, so that verily we know of other, shall I say, Shamballas which are far beyond the vistas and in magnitude to this one. In the higher spiritual dimensions in which the Logi, the Archangels and so on reside are far beyond the magnitude of conception in your third-dimensional minds. They would only confuse you to have such explanations given to you. In the freedom and liberation of your consciousness from the flesh, you will be able to better envision and to correctly interpolate such values into your consciousness so that they will not add confusion to such existing concepts which are rather burdensome in themselves sometimes; are they not? And so I, Maha Chohan, who am your very humble servant, along with all of us here in these great centers, have only your common interest at heart. We have only the greatest love, the greatest feeling of unison and in the expression of our unification, can we fully progress into the higher realms of consciousness.

Until such further transmissions, please do not hesitate to send us questions as we know in your moments of attunement and consciousness with us what is transpiring in your minds. For there is no separation in the spiritual worlds of consciousness even though you may think the dimensions of time or space are tremendous, as they are relegated into the concepts of space and time as they exist in your earth consciousness. And so we remain as always, your brothers and sisters in the Shamballas.

CHAPTER 57

Greetings, loved ones. I see that you are sitting presently in the great temple in the center of Aureleus, somewhere in the position where we previously discontinued our discussion. Also I would like to clear up what otherwise might be something of a small misunderstanding in the identity of this temple. As it was previously stated, it looked exactly like the temple of Solomon on the earth plane except for the beautiful crystalline structures and that it was the temple of Solomon. Now this is not quite correct because the name Solomon was merely used in that metaphor to so describe the earth-plane temple. The true name of this temple is the Temple of the Four Graces. They are the Grace of Goodness, the Grace of Charity, the Grace of Love and the Grace of Wisdom. Over the top of this great temple as you see is the beautiful white radiant dome which somewhat signifies the in-pouring nature of the all-pervading God Force. Now as Kung Fu would say, that wisdom like food, should not be eaten in haste or in anger but in contemplation, so that we too shall pause momentarily while we so digest what has previously been given and to so enlarge these abstract concepts so that they may better be digested by your minds.

My worthy teacher, Maha Chohan, gave you some description and some of the equations of time in our dimensional factors which related to your earth-plane dimensional factors. In other words, we could, as we have worked out a formula here for you, use the multiple of 100 as Plato expressed the 10,000-year period of the soul evolution. We will not say that Plato was wrong but say that Plato did not state entirely the absolute concept as it was evaluated into the spiritual dimensions. So we actually saw how the 10,000-year cycle of evolution developed into something like one million years. Now in your earth plane bibliography, you have a term which is frequently used among Christians and Bible students and that it is the 'gathering of the ten tribes'. Now many people have pictured the 'ten tribes' as some ten large groups of people living in tents or something of that nature, perhaps wigwams, out in the badlands or in the wilderness. Such is not the case. The 'ten tribes' properly interpreted means the ten ages of time which have existed since the Shamballa came upon your earth, nearly a million years ago. By the multiple of 100, you will see that the thousand, as it was signified in the interpretation of Revelation, referred to the millennium.

The word millennium itself not only means a long interval of time but means one million. Therefore, the one thousand which is termed the Millennium in your Revelations of the New Testament refers to a one-thousand year cycle as it might be expressed here, or in other words, one hundred thousand years in your earth-plane dimension. Each one of these one-hundred thousand years, as it is a cycle or an age, refers to all of the individuals who have lived on the earth at that particular cycle, so that in the final conclusion as it has been prophesied in your Bible, that in the return of these 'ten tribes', you will see through the process of reincarnation and spiritual evolution that each one of these individuals who has so lived in your earth plane at one of these dimensions and that as his vibration may be so integrated as to be completely relevant at this conclusion of this cycle, he will so again reincarnate into your earth plane dimension in the next interpretation of earth time as was so mentioned by the millennium concept of the Bible. Here again is another age of one hundred thousand years so that prophetically speaking, you can say that the spiritual age of your earth is and has already started into its new spiritual evolution which will last for one hundred thousand years.

Now do not expect me to give you time beyond this equation. It is not necessary at this time and I would not so confuse or confound your earth minds. Now in the evaluation of time and reincarnation as it has been so expressed in the numerous transcripts or explorations as have been given to you, to each individual he may have evolved some sort of a personal philosophy or concept. He may become either very spiritually lazy or that he may assume some sort of a hasty attitude. He may say, "Well, I have only three or four thousand years more to live and I have a lot to work out, I must hurry." Or he may say, "It is entirely irrelevant. I have whole ages before me." Now neither one of these assumptions is correct. While you may have a few thousand years to work out certain karmic conditions, yet as it has been previously explained there is neither judge nor jury who resides over you. You become your own master and in the mastership, you will either use the whip or you will use the light of Supreme Guidance, whichever you so determine for yourself. In the other equation, the individual may say, "I do not need to hurry. I can do what I want here because I have hundreds of thousands of years to work out these conditions later on. Perhaps too at that time I may be somewhat stronger." I may remind this individual of the story as it exists in some of the

451

texts in India and that there was a wonderful and wise adept who ascended into Nirvana and that in the full realization of this heavenly state of consciousness, he was full and complete with the wisdom of the immortal ages, so he said and proclaimed loudly to himself, "Now I am great and I have assumed all; my consciousness is complete and I have no need for such further continuance," and so that immediately he found himself in a low physical plane of evolution in which he suffered much pain and degradation. So you will see that there is a natural sequence of law or compensation or as it has been called, yoga. The law of cause and effect always works and that you in yourself express the fullest measure of that law of cause and effect. Until such further transmissions,

Gamaliel.

CHAPTER 58

(One month later.) Welcome back to Aureleus, dear ones, and we are most happy that you have made your adjustment and found your new home, a place which will serve and be to your liking. I believe we were somewhere in the vicinity of the temple of Solomon or shall I say, rather, the central temple which was copied by Solomon on your earth plane when we temporarily discontinued our transmissions.

So let us move over into another section which you saw previously and which is devoted to the Grecian time or the Hellenic arts as they existed in the field of philosophy during and after the time of such exponents of philosophy as Plato and Socrates. Now let us ascend these temple steps in this large and beautiful temple and that it looks to you something like glistening white marble, although it is the same beautiful crystal structures. As you see, there is a facade of columns which rise in graceful and slender proportions across the entire front of this temple. There are also wide and ample doorways and passageways into the central portions of this beautiful academy. This particular building is an exact replica of the academy which was used by Plato in Athens in the Grecian philosophical renaissance.

However, do not expect to see Plato here at this particular time. He does occasionally come to Aureleus but his services are rendered in another dimension in another teaching center which serves somewhat as our own Shamballa does in another part or another galaxy of the great celestial universe.

However, to best understand more of reincarnation and of such things as you have been pondering in your mind in the last few days which relate to the various astronomical structures of the universe, we will sit here beside the great central entrance of this beautiful academy building while you look about you and I will go further into the more pertinent facts which are relative to astronomy, astrophysics and concepts which deal with reincarnation. Up until the present time, your concept of the evolution through the various stages of man's reincarnation seems to be somewhat fixed in purpose as to Shamballa, or with the astral worlds which were served by the Shamballa. Such, however, is not the case.

Through the great terrestrial and celestial universe, there are other galaxies of stars which are also served by spiritual centers, some of which are larger and some of which are smaller than our own Shamballa. In the future in my discussion, I will refer to two different planes of consciousness or concept. As far as the planetary systems or the star galaxies are concerned, I will refer to them either as terrestrial: those which can be seen by the earth astronomer or by some such person with the physical eye, and the celestial solar system: those which exist in dimensions which are visible only to the clairvoyant. This is necessary because only a very small portion of the terrestrial and celestial universe is visible to the physical eye. Your earth astronomer with his latest reflectory and refractory telescopes can see about three hundred million stars of various magnitudes in the universe about him. He is also consciously aware of other universes beyond this universe. For our purpose at the present moment, we will confine our discussion to the immediate galaxy which is under the supervision and control of the Shamballa in a spiritual sense.

As you know from previous discussions that each sun or star, as it is sometimes called, that is visible to your physical eye must necessarily have its creation through a vortex of some celestial energies stemming from another dimension. This was explained to you in a previous transmission by Faraday. The great swirling masses of Radiant Energy in so precipitating themselves by the factor of centripetal force (for want of a better name) toward the center will manifest as a star. In our own galaxy of star clusters which is under our control, there are about two thousand various stars of different magnitudes. However, all of these stars or suns do not have solar systems. There are a few of this number which are still in somewhat of a state whereby they are either not capable of supporting a planetary system because of lack of sufficient intensity or radiating qualities, or they may be of such nebulous nature as to be insufficient in density that they may appear more as a cloud-like mass to the number of suns or stars which have the planetary systems; however, these will average about six planets which support life somewhat similar to your own earth plane. Now all of these planets are of course comparatively small in the vastness of the spaces about you and that to the most powerful telescopes on your earth, they would be completely invisible. Also, there are many of these planetary systems which do not exist in your own third-dimensional equation of mass and energy.

There are about seven different levels or dimensions which come directly under our supervision and control. These various thousands of planets in their different equations of mass or energy and in their respective dimensions, become the summerlands or the devachans or heavens as they have been described or the higher astral worlds as they are also known to you earth people. It has been hinted somewhat that these are the worlds in which the various artisans, craftsmen and people of your own world will in their evolution and reincarnation ascend into these different celestial worlds and thus maintain a continuity of their spiritual and material evolutions. In mentioning the number of three hundred million stars or suns of different magnitudes which are visible to your earth astronomer, may I say to him that this is only a small portion of the actual number of stars or suns which are in existence in the universe about you and that also this universe which you see about you in the Milky Way which stretches across the heavens is only one of a countless number of universes which stretch out into the vastness of what is called space.

Now it so happens that as I mentioned a few moments ago, that there are other healing and teaching centers which function and which somewhat resemble our own Shamballa and which serve their functional purposes with either a large or a small number of planetary systems in other parts of the great terrestrial and celestial universe, so that it becomes somewhat of a problem for your minds to conceive that an individual is not confined with a succession of evolutions or reincarnations into the higher spiritual planes which are served by our Shamballa. Neither is he confined by necessity in his higher stages of evolution to go through the various centers of the Shamballa as they are being described to you. He can and does so exercise his prerogative of will that he can transcend to other galaxies and star clusters of which there are an infinite number and existing in an infinite number of

456

dimensions. As it is with the various peoples who have at one time lived upon your earth plane, many of these are not found in the teaching centers of our Shamballa, neither are they found in the various higher astral worlds as they are serving in their reincarnations or evolutions in various capacities, or they are learning new and more pertinent facts relative to their existence in other galaxies and in other Shamballas throughout the great universes.

Now you are beginning to grasp somewhat in a small way the vastness, the scale and the magnitude of the infinity of God's plan which He has for you and in which you can spend a ceaseless eternity of time and never come to the end of the evolutions into different dimensions and into different times and into different places. I may assure you that in the future also a great deal of what I have somewhat summarized here in these few lines will be further enlarged and that you will be given much more information concerning these other galaxies and other portions of the universe.

The astronomer, who is peering through his telescope or he is taking pictures with the camera and that as he classifies the various stars or suns as he likes to call them sometimes, is only seeing a very small portion of his universe, that there are great suns which exist beyond the vision of his physical eye. When he becomes clairvoyant in a future day and develops such telescopes of such nature that they can peer into the other dimensions which are more relative to the celestial portions of his universe or to other universes, then he will begin to grasp the true meaning of what is meant by astronomy. The term astronomical figures will not suffice in this case. He will have to invent a whole new vocabulary of superlatives to describe these various and innumerable universes which he sees about him. The invisible world or the world of space will no longer exist. He will see space filled not only with the Radiant Energies but he will also see great suns and planetary systems of such size and of such magnitude that he will be staggered and dumbfounded. He will see planets which, like Eros, do not necessarily evolve into the simple shape of a spheroid but they can exist in innumerable shapes and sizes being somewhat like the pictures of the snowflakes which you have drawn in the various cataloguing of the various crystalline structures which exist on your earth plane surface. Can you imagine a planet which looks like a snowflake? And yet there are such. Do not confine your concept into such dimensions as involve the various familiar things which you see about you in your everyday walks of life because I can assure you, my dear ones, that there are things which exist in the heavens about you which defy your imagination.

There has also been a question posed here as to the qualitative and quantitative philosophies which might be expounded or portrayed in our visitations through the various centers of Aureleus as this planet and center is confined necessarily to the exploitation and the expounding of the various philosophical factors which have, and are, involved in the histories of your own earth planet as well as the many thousands of planets which are served by Shamballa. It occurs to the average individual that perhaps we here, as philosophers and knowing something of the philosophies of the earth, wish to expound some of the more familiar systems of such philosophies as they exist in the libraries of your earth. May I assure you, my friends, that most of us who have so expounded these theories on your earth plane are not necessarily proud of these works. We have long since ascended into such realms and dimensions where the books and the works, which we have left behind seem pitiful in comparison to that which we can glimpse about us. We will say and we will quote a familiar earth plane term, that the proof of the pudding is in the eating. In all logic and reasoning and the assumption of logic and wisdom within one's own mind is a derivation of principles and relationships which come as a natural and logical sequence of life about you, and that such derivations as they serve their time and place, are only relevant to the existence of life about you and as you pass on into other dimensions, such factors as you have previously so conceived will fall away from you and you assume a new perspective and your horizon is consequently expanded to a much more vast and larger proportion. Also may I remind you that our prime purpose in the exploration of the different centers of the Shamballa is for the purpose of acquainting you with the function and with the services which we are rendering to the lower astral worlds and to the terrestrial planets which exist in the different solar systems.

So, my friends, do not expect us to expound our personal philosophies and may I say that if we did so they would completely confound you and would be entirely irrelevant to your own earth plane existence. As you look about you and see the vastness, the magnitude, the beauty of all of this great city just as you have witnessed and have been a part of the daily life in other such centers of Shamballa in your tours and in your transmissions, so these too shall become small and insignificant in ascending into other realms and to other dimensions which far supersede these. We here are servants to the earth people and to the various terrestrial and celestial worlds and that in our services we are doing this gladly and with the foresight that with such suitable servitude and the incurrence of the wisdom and philosophies which such servitude brings into the realm and dimension of our consciousness that this will enable us to ascend into a higher dimension and thus become a greater servant for the all-pervading and all-permeating intelligence which manifests itself throughout all dimensions. Until such further time, however, my dear ones, may I remain your true brother in spirit.

Copernicus.

EPILOGUE

It is an obvious fact that the world has entered into a New Age. The last fifty years, and particularly since World War II, science has literally showered the people of the earth with innumerable inventions, contrivances, electronic and mechanical machines and appliances; and while these were all designed with an utilitarian purpose or were conceived to meet the increasing demands of a highly-competitive civilization, yet man, as a whole, has found this highly-developed technocracy vastly productive of certain repercussive elements in the transposition of life as it is being lived under this highly-mechanized age. The launching of the space satellites has literally brought man up to the threshold of open space; and while technically-speaking, this could indeed be heralded as a wonderful advent, yet psychologically speaking, has only added to these repercussive side effects. As a whole, man is adaptable to progressive ages only in sequences of evolutionary patterns which involve numerous lifetimes; and that so far as the average individual is concerned he will, just as he has always, adapt himself to new tenures of life only in such sequences of progressive lifetimes. Therefore, to the great masses of humanity which now swarm upon the surface of the planet earth, this sudden transition into a New Age has also brought with it a host of seemingly incurable and unalterable conditions which are the progeny of psychic pressures born and bred in the reactionary reaches of the subconscious mind.

As man is no more or less than he thinks, and that such thinking is an oscillating process with the subconscious, so that ultimately every man will express in some fashion the sum and total of these subconscious derivatives. Statistics reveal that mankind, as a whole, is in dire need of an entirely new and reconstructive philosophy of life which would primarily be based upon man's relationship with higher, interdimensional relationships, and to thus establish an equilibrium which would reestablish the individual upon a healthy pathway of life.

While in a general sense, the various religious orders and cultisms, as are existing at the present time, seem to offer to large segments of humanity these necessary equilibristic elements, yet a careful study will reveal that they are only temporary palliatives and engendered as escape mechanisms wherein the individual seeks to relieve these psychic pressures; yet these various psychic devices as expressions of hope, faith and courage, and the belief in various pantheisms of external spiritual forces do not, in any sense of the word, change the individual in his present position upon his personal pathway of evolution. Such changes take place only through a form of transcendency brought about through the junction of various cycular parallaxes, wherein he attains at least a partial, if not complete psychic rectification.

In order to attain such psychic or spiritual transcendency which will thus rectify subconscious or psychic malformations, the individual must not only acquaint himself with all the creative principles of life, but he must also become aware of his own evolutionary pattern. At the present time, the seeker is forced to wade through a vast and preponderant welter of ideologies, philosophies, and various derivations which only add to his confusion and despair. Moreover, none of these interpretations are supported either by the desired permanent results, nor is man made acquainted with his true evolutionary pattern of life. To fill in these and all other desired results which can be described as healing, mental, physical, and spiritual transcendency, proper evaluation of the past, present, and future as evolutionary patterns are all part of the Science of Life, called Unarius.

To begin to indoctrinate the seeker and to open up new avenues which have heretofore been unknown and hidden in his confusion, a factual philosophy of life can thereby be entered into which is neither a palliative nor an escape mechanism, but is a complete exposé of all generic principles of life and man's own personal position at the present moment.

This science begins with the presentation through a series of seven books called "The Pulse of Creation", designed as a bibliography for the future generations of mankind. These books and the adjunctive teaching course will place at the disposal of the seeker all of the known and presently unknown elements of life. Man will thus, in this proper evaluation, be able to not only relieve existing psychic pressures and their consequent physical and mental malfunctions, thus bringing about the required transcendency which will heal all abnormalities, replace confusion with a quiet calm, despair with complete realization, and link himself up with new cycles of spiritual transpositions which will infuse him with Radiant Energies; but will also give him power and dominion over all obstacles, a wise jurisprudence which will solve all conditions.

It is only fitting that in an epilogue of this nature some mention be given to those who were instrumental in bringing into the world this Monumental Spiritual Movement. As outlets for Unarius and cofounders of the first nucleus of the Science of Life, Ruth and Ernest Norman have not only set aside such small or large differences which involve the usual structures of the material world, such as personal differences of character and evaluations of life, financial and material appurtenances which are so customarily associated in the material dispensations, in so doing, have demonstrated to a miraculous degree, various adjustments in their own lives; but also to all who they have touched, incurred similar healings and adjustments.

Even in the writing of the books themselves, and particularly in regard to "The Voice of Eros" that this book was made possible only by the constant and diligent application of almost countless hours of composition upon a composing machine by Ruth, as an individual not accustomed, either by nature or training, to such exacting and monotonous mechanical regularities. These books, in themselves, bear silent tribute to one who has not only overcome but has put into actual practice the wisdom she has learned through this 'Science of Life'.

Moreover, the same, too, can be said in general principles, of Ernest and that as two individuals who are thus now collectively expressing themselves as outlets for Unarius, it must be remembered that this is the culmination of a thousand or more lifetimes and countless thousands of years of living and reliving and activating not only in the material worlds but also in the spiritual worlds, the basic and motivating principles of life such as are postulated in these works.

As Jesus said, "By their fruits ye shall know them", and at no time and in no age have two people so collectively and in such short time borne so much fruit. Only in the highly-developed clairvoyant aptitudes as have been demonstrated and currently expressed through Ernest, and with the completely dedicated purpose of fulfillment as expressed by Ruth, could such fruit have been brought to maturity. Nor could it be said that she lacks any of these necessary spiritual aptitudes, for she too, has demonstrated the highest degree and attainment of spiritual transcendencies and their subsequent progressive evaluations.

As was prophesied, the world is full of false prophets and teachers, those whose voices shout with empty promises and bear only the fruit of mockery; the empty echo of their voices reverberates back through the passages of time into the catacombs wherein are buried the skeletons of those who shouted similar promises so long ago.

Nor would we so have our voices mingled with those of these false prophets but let us speak to you in another way by first offering you the bowl filled with the fruit of attainment: let those who have also found this same fruit share it with you and that they have found in these works the necessary transforming elements which will also enable you to form all necessary junctions and attain your transcendency. Seek diligently, for "As ye seek so shall ye find" and surely as the Kingdom of Heaven is Within, and that in finding this Kingdom, all things are added unto you.

The Central Mind of Unarius—Sha-tok
(formerly known as Jesus of Nazareth)

Other works by Ernest L. Norman:

The Voice of Venus
The Voice of Hermes
The Voice of Orion
The Voice of Muse

The Infinite Concept of Cosmic Creation
Cosmic Continuum
Infinite Perspectus
Infinite Contact
Truth About Mars
The Elysium (Parables)
The Anthenium "
Magnetic Tape Lectures
Tempus Procedium
Tempus Invictus
Tempus Interludium Vols. I & II

Also a publication, now reprinted by
Unarius Publishing Company:
The True Life of Jesus of Nazareth (1899)

(The Sequel): The Story of the Little Red
Box